GALEN BURGHARDT
MORTON LANE
JOHN PAPA

with the assistance of:
ROBERT GRISWOLD *and* GEOFFREY LUCE

THE
TREASURY
BOND
BASIS

AN IN-DEPTH
ANALYSIS FOR HEDGERS,
SPECULATORS AND
ARBITRAGEURS

Probus Publishing Company
Chicago, Illinois

Library of Congress Cataloging-in-Publication Data

Burghardt, Galen.
    Treasury bond basis trading.

    Includes index.
    1. Hedging (finance) 2. Government securities—
United States.   3. Futures—United States.   I. Lane,
Morton N.   II. Papa, John.   III. Title.
HG6041.B78 1989 332.63'232   88-32334

ISBN 1-55738-050-3

Printed in the United States of America

        3   4   5   6   7   8   9   0

Contents

Contents

Preface

Our aim when we began this book was to provide newcomers to the Treasury bond futures market with a primer on the price relationship between T-bonds and T-bond futures. To this end, Bob Griswold, as an intern in our research group, was given the task of putting together an introduction to the Treasury bond basis that would answer basic questions such as "What is it?" and "What does it mean to buy or sell the basis?"

It soon became apparent, however, that a primer could not convey the richness of the Treasury bond futures contract and would ignore most of the contract's history. Bond futures have been trading for only 11 years, but we are already seeing a second generation of traders enter the market, many of whom could benefit from an accounting of how the contract came to behave as it does. Furthermore, as of this writing, we are approaching what may be the end of the longest economic expansion since the end of World War II. Economic turning points produce unusual interest rate settings, and in this case we might encounter a negatively sloped yield curve, but without the extreme volatility and turmoil that accompanied Volcker's great monetary experiment in the early 1980's. If so, the Treasury bond basis is likely to behave differently from the way it has previously and anyone who trades the basis or uses bond futures to hedge should be prepared to understand why.

What began as a simple primer, then, has become this book; and its preparation owes a great deal to the contributions of several past and present employees of Discount Corporation of New York Futures. First, I would like to acknowledge Michael Berg, who was responsible for our Chicago Board of Trade operation in the early 1980's. He and I spent several weekends trying to solve the puzzle of the behavior of T-bond deliveries. It was during these sessions that we encountered the wild card trade. Our report to clients on that trade became the basis of Discount Corporation's "Blue Book," which was compiled with Vir Doshi's help and was used widely as a primer for analyzing cash/futures relationships in all financial futures contracts.

Michael's place at the Board of Trade was taken by Bob Palazola, who, with Dennis Malec, helped us understand the hedging implications of the contract's behavior. Ed Landers, Linda Reynolds, and Craig Zucker have also made their contributions.

More recently, David Emanuel evaluated the distinctions between the Treasury bond futures that were listed in Sydney, London, and Chicago. His work led to a finer appreciation of the value of the short's various delivery options, and much of that work is contained in this volume. It was Jeff Kleban who brought the switch option to our attention and who has helped us unravel the intricacies of that trade.

Galen Burghardt has pulled the various threads together in this book, using his analytic abilities to clarify my occasionally woolly thinking. Apart from that, he put his own stamp on the book with his extensions of the rules of thumb relating to duration and yield to the cheapest to deliver. That work is reflected in our portrayal of shifting deliverables and, in a related field, in our understanding of options on bond futures.

All of this theorizing would have been far less valuable without the considerable practical experience of John Papa. John has executed basis trades on our clients' behalf for several years and is one of the most experienced basis traders in the business.

Finally, there were several people who helped to keep us honest and who provided many of the raw materials for this book. Michael Hughes, who monitors the basis daily for his clients, read several drafts and made many improvements. Further, without Michael and Liz Stump, we would not have a running record of cash market prices that correspond to the daily close of the futures market. Vir Doshi is responsible for most of the programs that allow us to analyze the basis and to anticipate likely shifts in the cheapest to deliver. John Gury put together a complete history of bond and note deliveries at the Chicago Board of Trade and contributed greatly to the graphics, especially in the chapter on the four eras of the bond basis. Cheryl Catlin put together most of the tables and several of the graphics. Geoffrey Luce, another intern in the research group, played a vital role. His careful and enthusiastic reading of the text, tables, and charts brought this project to a close much sooner and in much better shape than could have been done without him.

As I write these acknowledgements, I realize how much has been contributed by so many people over the years. We have not always been the first to take advantage of shifts in the way the bond basis behaves, but we have been vigorous in our pursuit of understanding why such shifts have taken place. This pursuit has allowed us to take advantage of opportunities well before they have disappeared altogether. The detective work has been both profitable and fun.

Morton Lane

Introduction

The Treasury Bond Basis

When Tom Wolfe created a bond trader as the lead character in his novel *The Bonfire of the Vanities*, he elevated bond traders to the glamorous ranks of test pilots and astronauts. Bond trading in general and Treasury bond trading in particular has become big business. The trades are huge and the risks enormous.

It was not always so. The glamor and excitement of bond trading is something that has emerged over the past decade, thanks in part to the Treasury's voracious appetite for borrowed money and in part to the emergence of Treasury bond futures.

Growth of the Treasury Bond Market

Although the U.S. Treasury has borrowed regularly in the long-term credit market since 1790, the Treasury's first offering of what we would recognize as a long bond was a 6-percent, no call, 20-year issue for $25 million in 1861.

Since then, the market for U.S. Treasury long bonds has grown in fits and starts, usually hitting its stride during major armed conflicts. By the end of World War II, the value of Treasury bonds that had at least 10 years remaining to maturity was just over $30 billion. Today, after two more wars and several peace-time years of more or less wanton borrowing, the value of Treasury long bonds in the public's hands has ballooned to $300 billion.

At the same time, in part because of raw growth in the size of the Treasury market and in part because of the volatility that interest rates have displayed since the late 1970s, the bond market has been transformed from a place in which trading was an accommodation for investors to a world in which $15 billion regularly turns over in the course of a trading day.

Growth of Treasury Bond Futures

When compared with the cash market for Treasury bonds, which have a long and rich heritage, the market for Treasury bond futures seems young and brash. The Chicago Board of Trade opened trading in Treasury Bond Futures on August 22, 1977. Within the fairly close fraternity of primary government securities dealers, the initial reaction to the new futures contract was a mixture of loathing and disdain. In Washington, D.C., the reaction at the Treasury and the Federal Reserve was a mixture of suspicion and grudging acceptance.

Since then, the market for Treasury bond futures has matured at a breathtaking pace. Today, the volume of trading often exceeds 400,000 contracts a day. At $100,000 par value of bonds per contract, this translates into the equivalent of $40 billion a day in bonds. Outstanding positions (open interest) in Treasury bond futures is just under 500,000 contracts, which represents about $50 billion in long-term Treasury bonds.

In a nutshell, the market is huge.

Who Uses the Futures Market?
As the book's title suggests, the Treasury bond futures market offers something for every kind of player: hedgers, speculators, and arbitrageurs.

The clearing membership of the Chicago Board of Trade reads like a *Who's Who* of the country's banks, investment banking houses, and primary government securities dealers. What they use the futures contract for runs the gamut of possibilities. For primary government securities dealers, the futures represent a ready outlet for laying off the risk in bidding for and distributing the huge waves of Treasury bonds that are auctioned off each quarter.

We also know that collectively, primary dealers maintain a massive short basis position. That is, they are short several billions of bonds and long roughly the same amount of futures. Our own reckoning of the dealers' gross income from this position is between $100 million and $200 million a year.

From *Pensions and Investment Age* (March 21, 1988), we find that many of the country's large pension funds and money managers use fixed income futures as part of their investment strategy. A very partial listing of those pension funds includes
- Amoco
- Bechtel
- DuPont
- Exxon
- Ford
- General Electric
- Honeywell
- IBM
- MMM
- Navistar
- Standard Oil
- USX
- World Bank

In other words, the players in this market are legitimate heavy hitters.

A Whole Book on the Bond Basis?

The Treasury bond basis ties the bond market to the futures market What makes the Treasury bond basis interesting is the combined complexity of the cash market for Treasury bonds and the structure of the futures contract. The Treasury bond market is made up of bonds bearing a wide range of coupons and maturities and different call provisions. Thus, even though Treasury bonds all share the same creditworthiness, the bonds themselves are different enough to make the market interesting. Also, the futures contract is designed so that the trader who is short the futures has several strategic delivery options that affect both what bond is delivered and when.

Taken together, the richness of the bond market and the diversity of the short's strategic options add up to a full book on the subject of the bond basis.

Thus, whether you are a hedger, a speculator, or an arbitrageur in the Treasury market, you should know all the ins and outs of the futures market.

Understanding the Bond Basis
Understanding the relationship between cash bonds and bond futures requires answers to a host of questions.
- What is the bond basis?
- How does the basis behave?
- How can selling the basis make money?
- What are the risks?
- Why would anyone ever want to be long the basis?
- How can portfolio managers benefit from trading the basis?

This book gives you the answers to all of these questions and more.

Organization of the Book

What Is the Bond Basis?
The first step is to assemble a set of tools, which we do in the Chapter 1. We define the basis, explain how the futures contract works, and lay out the transactions and financing involved in taking long and short positions in the basis.

How Does It Behave?

How the basis behaves is a complex problem that occupies most of this book. In Chapter 2 we tackle the question of how the futures price is tied to the prices of actual Treasury bonds. In practice, from the perspective of whoever is short the futures contract, this entails finding the "cheapest bond to deliver" and deciding when to deliver it. What makes this problem so interesting is that the "short" (that is, the person who is short the futures contract) has roughly 30 bonds to choose from and a full month in which delivery can be made.

In this chapter, we show how the cheapest to deliver is affected by changes in the level of yields and how the timing decision is affected by the slope of the yield curve.

A close examination of the short's rights to pick both the bond and the delivery day reveals a variety of options that stem from peculiarities of the futures contract and the market for government securities. In Chapter 3 we look more closely at these options, which include the "wild card," the "switch option," and the "timing option."

Theory is fine, but every course of action based on theory encounters problems in the real world. In Chapter 4, we spell out some of the practical considerations that anyone who trades the basis must know and understand. For example, as the dealers discovered in an especially painful episode in 1986, there can be massive "short squeezes." There can be minor short squeezes that are nevertheless enough to break the trade. Short-term financing in the "repo" market is not a homogeneous financial commodity, but depends instead of whether the bond being financed is "general collateral" or "on special." Further, a basis position in the delivery month is a different creature from a basis position outside the delivery month, and the basis trader should be aware of the alternatives in each case.

How the basis has behaved is covered in Chapter 5 and Chapter 6. In Chapter 5 we take you through the broad developments in basis trading that have taken place since bond futures started trading in the 1970s. In Chapter 6 we take you step-by-step through the four quarterly delivery cycles for 1987. For someone studying the basis, 1987 was an especially good year because changes in the level of yields produced several changes in the cheapest to deliver.

The Note Basis

Although most of this book focuses on the basis in bond futures, there are futures contracts on both 5-year and 10-year Treasury notes as well. Chapter 7 is devoted to a brief discussion of how the note basis behaves. The financial forces that drive the note basis are the same as those that drive the bond basis, but for the most part the effects are smaller.

Applications for Portfolio Managers

Chapter 8 brings us back to the question of why the primary government securities dealers have been short the basis over the past few years. Presumably the position has been a profitable one. If so, any portfolio manager with a natural long position in longer-term government securities may be able to profit from the same trade by replacing long bonds with long futures. The trade is effectively the same as selling the basis and can substantially enhance the yield of a Treasury securities portfolio.

We also touch on the implications of cheap futures for hedgers.

Caveat

This book will give you most of what you need to understand the bond basis. What you will not find here is a detailed description of the U.S. Treasury bond market and of how those bonds are priced. If you are approaching the Treasury market as a novice, you will benefit from such useful resources as Frank Fabozzi's *Handbook of Treasury Securities* (Probus Publishing, 1987).

Chapter 1

Basic Concepts

"Basis" is a term common to all futures contracts. For example, the difference between the price of wheat today (its *spot price*) and its futures price is the *wheat basis*. Because the wheat futures market is competitive, the wheat basis tends to equilibrate the cost of financing and storing wheat until the future delivery date. To make it worth anyone's while to set aside wheat for future delivery, the futures price of wheat must be higher than the spot price of wheat. As a result, the wheat basis typically is negative.

Bonds can be set aside for future delivery as well. The chief differences between bonds and wheat are in the physical costs of storage and in what is often called convenience yield. U.S. Treasury bonds are nearly all held in electronic book entry form with the Federal Reserve; thus, the physical costs of storage for them are zero. Additionally, bonds throw off a yield in the form of actual or accrued coupon income that works to offset the cost of financing the bond until future delivery.

Moreover, if the yield curve is positively sloped so that long-term interest rates are higher than short-term interest rates, holding a bond position for future delivery actually produces a net income rather than a net outgo. For this reason and other reasons explored in this book, the futures price of a Treasury bond tends to be lower than the spot price; the bond basis tends to be positive.

There is one more striking similarity between wheat and bonds. Not all wheat is the same. There are slight differences in quality, and wheat from Kansas is not the same (because of transportation costs if nothing else) as wheat from Nebraska. Nevertheless, wheat futures contracts allow for the delivery of different grades of wheat in different locations. Also, it is the person who is short the futures contract who decides what to deliver and where. As a result, the wheat basis is geared to the grade of wheat and location that combine to make the cost of delivering wheat into the futures contract as low as it can be. That is, the wheat futures price is driven by the "cheapest to deliver."

So it is with bonds. The physical location of bonds is irrelevant, but the Treasury bond futures contract allows the delivery of any U.S. Treasury bond that has at least 15 years to first call. Currently, there are more than 30 such bonds, each with its own coupon, maturity, and in some cases, call date. These coupon and maturity differences make up the different grades of bonds. Much of the challenge in understanding the bond basis is in understanding what makes a bond cheap to deliver. The rest of the challenge is in understanding when it is best to make delivery.

This chapter lays out the basic tools needed for an understanding of the bond basis. In particular, it addresses the following topics:

- definition of the bond basis
- conversion factors
- futures invoice price
- carry, the profit or loss of holding bonds
- implied repo rate
- RP versus reverse RP rates
- buying and selling the basis
- an idealized strategy for trading the bond basis

Definition of the Bond Basis

A bond's basis is the difference between its cash price and the product of the futures price and the bond's conversion factor:

$$B = P - (F \times C)$$

where

B	is the basis for the bond/futures combination
P	is the spot or cash bond price per $100 face value of the bond
F	is the futures price per $100 face value of the futures contract
C	is the conversion factor for the bond

Units

Bond and bond futures prices typically are quoted for $100 face value and the prices themselves are stated in full points and 32nds of full points. In practice, the 32nds are broken down further into 64ths for bonds that are traded actively and in size, but the conventional quote is still in 32nds with the 64ths represented by a "+."

The 32nds are represented differently in different places. In *The Wall Street Journal*, for example, the 32nds are set off from the whole points by a dash. That is, 91 and 14/32nds would appear as 91—14. Occasionally, you will find the 32nds stated explicitly as 91—14/32nds. Also, because of programming and formatting problems, the dash may be replaced by a period, so that 91—14 appears as 91.14. In this book, the 32nds are stated, for the sake of clarity.

Conversion factors are expressed in decimal form.

Important Point   In practice, all prices are converted first to decimal form. The resulting basis, which is then in decimal form, is converted into 32nds simply by multiplying the decimal basis by 32.

Basis Comparison

Table 1.1 shows the bases in 32nds of the 31 bonds that were eligible for delivery into the Chicago Board of Trade March 1988 contract on February 19, 1988.

Table 1.1 Deliverable Bonds (2/19/88)

Delivery Month = March 1988
RP Rate = 6.650%
March Bond Futures = 93 - 22/32nds

Trade Date = 2/19/88
Settlement Date = 2/22/88

First Delivery Date = 3/01/88 (Days Remaining = 8)
Futures Expiration Date = 3/22/88 (Days Remaining = 29)
Last Delivery Date = 3/31/88 (Days remaining = 38)

COUPON (1)	MATURITY (2)	CASH PRICE 2/19/88 (3)	CONVERSION FACTOR (4)	BASIS (5)	YIELD (6)	YIELD VALUE OF 32ND (7)	DOLLAR VALUE OF BASIS PT. (8)	DURATION (9)	CASH PRICE +ACCRUED INTEREST (10)	CARRY DOLLARS PER DAY (11)	CARRY 32nds PER DAY (12)	TOTAL CARRY 32nds/DAY TO LAST DELIVERY DAY (13)	IMPLIED RP RATE TO FIRST DELIVERY DAY (14)	IMPLIED RP RATE TO FUTURES EXPIRATION (15)	IMPLIED RP RATE TO LAST DELIVERY DAY (16)
10.750	05/15/03	118.01	1.2378	66	8.601	0.00329	94.93	8.19	120.9550	71.90	0.230	8.743	-68.06	-12.43	-7.41
11.125	08/15/03	121.12	1.2723	70	8.601	0.00320	97.73	8.38	121.5689	81.03	0.259	9.853	-71.52	-13.20	-7.93
11.875	11/15/03	127.21	1.3408	65	8.826	0.00305	102.30	8.15	130.8860	84.46	0.270	10.270	-61.19	-10.40	-5.82
12.375	05/15/04	132.12	1.3910	66	8.827	0.00292	106.92	8.22	135.7407	89.23	0.286	10.850	-59.16	-9.81	-5.36
13.750	08/15/04	145.00	1.5175	91	8.594	0.00269	115.97	8.33	145.2644	109.41	0.350	13.304	-78.31	-14.84	-9.12
11.625	11/15/04	126.08	1.3289	56	8.828	0.00299	104.63	8.43	129.4117	80.32	0.257	9.766	-51.95	-7.91	-3.94
12.000	05/15/05	130.04	1.3682	62	8.810	0.00287	108.80	8.51	133.3887	83.27	0.266	10.128	-56.64	-9.20	-4.92
10.750	08/15/05	118.28	1.2548	41	8.844	0.00307	101.81	8.92	119.0192	75.47	0.242	9.178	-36.19	-4.36	-1.22
9.375	02/15/06	107.26	1.1289	66	8.518	0.00324	96.51	9.32	107.9928	58.07	0.186	7.061	-76.81	-14.99	-9.41
8.375	08/15/08-03	97.30	1.0325	39	8.590	0.00332	94.11	10.00	98.0986	48.87	0.156	5.943	-48.86	-6.83	-3.22
8.750	11/15/08-03	101.08	1.0660	44	8.601	0.00363	86.18	8.67	103.6298	48.96	0.157	5.953	-51.56	-8.19	-4.28
9.125	05/15/09-04	104.10	1.1005	39	8.624	0.00350	89.26	8.72	106.7943	53.41	0.171	6.495	-42.54	-5.63	-2.30
10.375	11/15/09-04	114.27	1.2155	31	8.674	0.00322	97.01	8.60	117.6655	67.67	0.217	8.229	-28.27	-1.50	0.91

Table 1.1 Deliverable Bonds (2/19/88) continued

Coupon	Maturity														
11.750	02/15/10-05	127.12	1.3425	51	8.645	0.00295	105.97	8.66	127.6010	87.09	0.279	10.591	-47.33	-6.48	-2.79
10.000	05/15/10-05	111.30	1.1841	32	8.652	0.00324	96.60	8.79	114.6573	62.83	0.201	7.652	-30.73	-2.25	0.32
12.750	11/15/10-05	138.27	1.4433	52	8.846	0.00273	114.57	8.52	140.3115	91.09	0.291	11.078	-43.14	-5.41	-2.01
13.875	05/15/11-06	147.25	1.5554	66	8.824	0.00253	123.73	8.52	151.5549	101.23	0.324	12.309	-52.13	-7.64	-3.85
14.000	11/15/11-06	149.14	1.5743	82	8.827	0.00247	126.48	8.61	153.2452	101.54	0.325	12.347	-48.11	-6.75	-3.02
10.375	11/15/12-07	116.02	1.2326	19	8.660	0.00297	105.37	9.25	118.8843	65.42	0.208	7.955	-13.47	2.52	3.96
12.000	08/15/13-08	131.30	1.3978	32	8.848	0.00263	118.72	9.37	132.1683	85.53	0.274	10.400	-25.09	-0.44	1.79
13.250	05/15/14-09	144.19	1.5299	40	8.630	0.00240	130.23	9.17	148.1975	90.26	0.269	10.975	-29.48	-1.75	0.78
12.500	08/15/14-09	137.23	1.4560	42	8.815	0.00249	125.74	9.51	137.9591	88.57	0.283	10.770	-33.79	-2.85	-0.06
11.750	11/15/14-09	130.16	1.3820	33	8.818	0.00259	120.84	9.43	133.6957	75.84	0.243	9.222	-25.80	-0.84	1.41
11.250	02/15/15	128.18	1.3561	48	8.528	0.00241	129.77	10.51	128.7788	71.18	0.228	8.656	-44.25	-5.97	-2.51
10.625	08/15/15	122.17	1.2892	56	8.494	0.00249	125.57	10.67	122.7356	65.18	0.209	7.925	-55.60	-9.15	-4.96
9.875	11/15/15	114.09	1.2073	38	8.522	0.00264	118.39	10.55	116.0670	55.23	0.177	6.716	-36.78	-4.12	-1.17
9.250	02/15/16	107.24	1.1383	35	8.519	0.00277	112.89	10.91	107.9279	54.75	0.175	6.658	-37.64	-4.28	-1.25
7.250	05/15/16	86.24	0.9167	28	8.492	0.00330	94.72	11.13	88.7218	35.29	0.113	4.291	-35.90	-4.07	-1.19
7.500	11/15/16	89.15	0.9442	32	8.482	0.00320	97.62	11.12	91.5086	37.01	0.116	4.500	-41.54	-5.60	-2.38
8.750	05/15/17	102.25	1.0841	39	8.489	0.00284	110.00	10.90	105.1611	46.13	0.148	5.609	-43.77	-6.13	-2.74
8.875	08/15/17	104.23	1.0981	59	8.438	0.00278	112.46	11.17	104.8894	50.06	0.160	6.088	-70.62	-13.44	-8.28

NOTE: 2.00 PM (CBT) CASH PRICES ARE MARKED BETWEEN THE BID AND OFFER
YIELDS ARE CALCULATED TO MATURITY FOR DISCOUNT SECURITIES AND TO THE CALL DATE FOR PREMIUM SECURITIES.
COST OF CARRY IS PER $1 MILLION FACE VALUE, AND IS SHOWN AS $/DAY, 32nd/DAY AND TOTAL TO LAST DELIVERY DATE IN 32nds.
COURTESY OF DCNYF RESEARCH GROUP.

Conversion Factors

The Chicago Board of Trade U.S. Treasury Bond contract allows for the delivery of $100,000 of any U.S. Treasury Bond that has at least 15 years remaining to maturity, or first call, if callable. With the wide range of bonds available for delivery, the Board of Trade uses *conversion factors* in the invoicing process to equate these bonds. Table 1.2 shows the conversion factors of all bonds that were eligible for delivery as of February 19, 1988 for contract months through March 1990.

The conversion factor is the approximate price, in decimals, at which the bond would yield 8 percent to maturity (rounded to whole quarters), or to first call if callable. It can be viewed as the approximate decimal price at which the bond would trade if it yielded 8 percent to first call. For example, the March 1988 conversion factor for the 8-7/8s of 2017 was 1.0981, which would correspond to a decimal price of 109.81, or a price of 109.26 (109-26/32nds) in conventional form.

Consider, for example, the 8-7/8s of 8/15/17. For the March 1988 contract, the conversion factor for this bond was set at 1.0981. On January 21, 1988, there were 29 years, 6 months, and 24 days left until expiration. The Chicago Board of Trade rounds this number to the number of whole quarters remaining from the first day of the delivery month (3/1/88) until expiration, truncating the odd days, leaving 29 years and 3 months. For example, 29 years, 6 months, and 24 days taken to expiration unrounded yields a theoretical conversion factor of 1.0986.

Characteristics of Conversion Factors
- Conversion factors are unique to each bond *and* to each delivery month.
- Conversion factors are constant throughout the delivery cycle.
- Conversion factors are used to calculate the invoice price of bonds delivered into the CBOT T-bond futures contracts.
- If the coupon > 8 percent—conversion factor > 1
  If the coupon < 8 percent—conversion factor < 1

- Conversion factor is the approximate number of futures contracts needed to be short to hedge every $100,000 par value long cash bonds if the bond is similar to the deliverable bond.

Futures Invoice Price

When a bond is delivered into the CBOT T-bond contract, the receiver of the bond pays the short an invoice price equal to the futures price times the conversion factor of the bond chosen by the short plus any accrued interest on the bond:

Invoice Price = (F × C) + AI

= (Futures Price × Conversion Factor) +
Accrued Interest

Accrued interest (AI) is also expressed per $100 face value of the bond.

Suppose, for example, that the 8-7/8s of 8/15/17 are delivered on 3/31/88 at a futures price of 92-07/32nds. The bond's conversion factor would be 1.0981 and accrued interest would be $1.09718. Accrued interest is calculated from the last coupon payment date (2/15/88) to 3/31/88. Thus, the invoice price would be

Invoice Price = (92.21875 × 1.0981) + 1.09718
= 102.36259

The futures contract calls for the delivery of $100,000 face value of bonds. For each futures contract, then, the total dollar amount of the invoice would be

Invoice Amount = $1000 × 102.36259
= $102,362.59

Example: Basis Calculation   Consider the 9-1/4s of 2/15/16. The conversion factor for this bond during the March 1988 delivery cycle is 1.1383. On February 19, 1988, at 2 p.m. Chicago time, it was trading in the cash market at 107-24/32nds, while the futures price on that day was 93-22/32nds. Recall that the basis is defined as

Basis = Cash Price − Futures Price × Conversion Factor

To calculate the basis, convert cash and futures prices into decimals.

$$\text{Basis} = 107.75 - 93.6875 \times 1.1383$$
$$= 1.1055$$

which is the basis in decimal form. Convert the result back to 32nds to get 35.38, which is simply rounded to 35 (see Table 1.1).

Carry: Profit or Loss of Holding Bonds

The price at which you would be willing to hold a bond for future delivery depends critically on what you will make or lose in interest while holding the bond.

Carry is the difference between the coupon income you make by holding the bond and what you pay to finance the bond. If carry is positive, as it will be if the yield curve is positively sloped, you earn interest income holding a bond for future delivery. If carry is negative, as it will be if the yield curve is negatively sloped, you lose interest income.

For various purposes, we find it useful to distinguish between
- daily carry in dollars
- carry in 32nds
- total carry in 32nds

Table 1.1 shows these three values in columns 11, 12, and 13, respectively, for each deliverable bond.

Daily Carry

The following formula gives carry in dollars per day for each $100 par value of the bonds.

Daily Carry = Daily Coupon Income − Daily Financing Cost

where:

Daily Coupon Income = [(I/2)/Days]

is based on the face value of the bond and

Daily Financing Cost = [(P + AI) × (RP/100)]/360

is based on the market value of the bond. The symbols used are these:

I	is the annual coupon, which is stated in full percentage points and which is divided by 2 to put it on a semi-annual basis.
Days	is the number of days between coupon payments and ranges between 181 and 186, so that coupon income works on a 365-day year.
P	is the market price per $100 face value of the bonds.
AI	is accrued interest per $100 face value of the bonds.
RP	is the repo rate for the bond, which is stated in full percentage points and is divided by 100 to restate in percent. The RP rate is the rate at which the bond is financed, can be overnight or term, and can be different for different bonds.
360	is the assumed number of days in a year for RP calculations.

Example: Carry Calculation   Consider the 8-7/8s of 8/15/17 on February 19, 1988. This bond's conversion factor for the March delivery cycle was 1.0981. Its price plus accrued interest was $104.8894 (see column 10 of Table 1.1), the RP rate was 6.650 percent, and the number of days between coupons, which for this bond are paid on February 15 and August 15, was 182. Given these particulars, we have:

Daily Coupon Income   = [(8.875/2)/182]
                                    = $0.02438187

Daily Financing Cost   = [$104.8894 × (6.650/100)]/360
                                    = $0.01937540

so that daily carry is

Daily Carry   = $0.02438187 − $.01937540
                = $0.0050060

or half a cent a day for each $100 face value of bonds. For $1 million face value of the 8-7/8s, daily carry in dollars would be:

Daily Carry   = 10,000 × $.0050060
                = $50.06

which you can find in column 11.

Carry in 32nds

Standard bond trading practice is to state carry in 32nds. The value of a 32nd for $1,000,000 par value of a bond is $312.50. Thus, daily carry in 32nds is found simply by dividing daily carry in dollars by $312.50. For the carry calculation example, where daily carry was $50.06, daily carry in 32nds would be:

Daily Carry in 32nds   = $50.06/$312.50
                         = 0.160/32nds

(See Table 1.1, column 12.)

Total Carry in 32nds

For the sake of convenience, carry is calculated for various holding periods. Total carry can be calculated to the first delivery day, futures expiration day, or to the last delivery day. Of the three, however, the example being developed shows only total carry to the last delivery

Table 1.2   Conversion Factors for Deliverable Bonds for Various Contracts Months

Coupon	Maturity	Mar 88	Jun 88	Sep 88	Dec 88	Mar 89	Jun 89	Sep 89	Dec 89	Mar 90
10-3/4%	5/15/03	1.2378								
11-1/8%	8/15/03	1.2723	1.2702							
8-3/8%	8/15/08-03	1.0325	1.0324							
11-7/8%	11/15/03	1.3408	1.3376	1.3350						
8-3/4%	11/15/08-03	1.0660	1.0652	1.0648						
12-3/8%	5/15/04	1.3910	1.3876	1.3847	1.3812	1.3783				
9-1/8%	5/15/09-04	1.1005	1.0995	1.0989	1.0979	1.0973				
13-3/4%	8/15/04	1.5175	1.5139	1.5095	1.5057	1.5011	1.4971			
11-5/8%	11/15/04	1.3289	1.3262	1.3240	1.3211	1.3188	1.3158	1.3134		
10-3/8%	11/15/09-04	1.2155	1.2136	1.2122	1.2103	1.2089	1.2069	1.2053		
11-3/4%	2/15/10-05	1.3425	1.3403	1.3374	1.3351	1.3322	1.3298	1.3267	1.3242	
12%	5/15/05	1.3682	1.3653	1.3630	1.3599	1.3575	1.3544	1.3518	1.3485	1.3458
10%	5/15/10-05	1.1841	1.1826	1.1815	1.1799	1.1787	1.1771	1.1759	1.1742	1.1729
10-3/4%	8/15/05	1.2546	1.2532	1.2511	1.2495	1.2474	1.2458	1.2436	1.2418	1.2396
12-3/4%	11/15/10-05	1.4433	1.4400	1.4373	1.4339	1.4310	1.4275	1.4245	1.4208	1.4177
9-3/8%	2/15/06	1.1289	1.1283	1.1272	1.1266	1.1255	1.1248	1.1236	1.1229	1.1217
13-7/8%	5/15/11-06	1.5554	1.5515	1.5483	1.5442	1.5408	1.5367	1.5331	1.5288	1.5250
14%	11/15/11-06	1.5743	1.5705	1.5672	1.5633	1.5599	1.5558	1.5523	1.5481	1.5444
10-3/8%	11/15/12-07	1.2326	1.2310	1.2300	1.2284	1.2273	1.2257	1.2245	1.2228	1.2216
12%	8/15/13-08	1.3976	1.3959	1.3935	1.3917	1.3893	1.3874	1.3848	1.3829	1.3802
13-1/4%	5/15/14-09	1.5299	1.5270	1.5248	1.5219	1.5196	1.5165	1.5141	1.5110	1.5084
12-1/2%	8/15/14-09	1.4560	1.4542	1.4517	1.4498	1.4473	1.4453	1.4427	1.4407	1.4379
11-3/4%	11/15/14-09	1.3820	1.3799	1.3785	1.3764	1.3749	1.3727	1.3711	1.3689	1.3672
11-1/4%	2/15/15	1.3561	1.3554	1.3541	1.3534	1.3521	1.3513	1.3499	1.3491	1.3477
10-5/8%	8/15/15	1.2892	1.2887	1.2876	1.2871	1.2860	1.2854	1.2843	1.2837	1.2826
9-7/8%	11/15/15	1.2073	1.2065	1.2062	1.2054	1.2051	1.2042	1.2039	1.2030	1.2027
9-1/4%	2/15/16	1.1383	1.1382	1.1376	1.1375	1.1369	1.1367	1.1361	1.1359	1.1353
7-1/4%	5/15/16	0.9167	0.9167	0.9171	0.9171	0.9175	0.9176	0.9180	0.9180	0.9184
7-1/2%	11/15/16	0.9442	0.9441	0.9445	0.9444	0.9447	0.9450	0.9450	0.9453	0.9453
8-3/4%	5/15/17	1.0841	1.0837	1.0837	1.0833	1.0833	1.0829	1.0829	1.0825	1.0825
8-7/8%	8/15/17	1.0981	1.0981	1.0977	1.0977	1.0972	1.0972	1.0968	1.0967	1.0963

* Bonds listed in order of first call date.

day, which is the optimal delivery date given positive carry and which is shown in Table 1.1, column 13. Chapter 2 deals with the problem of optimal delivery date.

For these calculations, total carry is daily carry multiplied by the number of days the bond is held. However, this number is only an approximation. If there is a coupon date between the time of calculation and the delivery date, the number of days between coupon periods changes slightly, thus changing the actual daily carry. An exact solution can be found by calculating the daily carry for each period, and multiplying by the number of days carried in the respective periods.

Theoretical Bond Basis

If there were only one bond available for delivery, or if there were never any question about what the deliverable bond would be or when the bond would be delivered, the bond basis would be very easy to figure. To simplify matters still more, suppose the bond in question bears an 8-percent coupon, so that its conversion factor is 1.000. In such a simple setting, the futures price would be approximately

Futures Price = Bond Price − Total Carry to Delivery

Because the bond's conversion factor is 1.000, the bond's basis in this case is just the difference between the bond's price and the futures price. If we take this difference, we find that

Basis   = Bond Price − Futures Price
           = Bond Price − (Bond Price − Total Carry)
           = Total Carry

Total carry, of course, has two parts. The first is daily carry in 32nds, which depends both on the difference between the RP rate and the bond yield and on the price of the bond. The second is the total number of days to delivery. Taking the two together produces a relationship between a bond's basis and the time to delivery like that shown in Chart

1.1. Chart 1.1 illustrates three key points given the following simplify-
ing assumptions:

- the height of the curve is total carry to delivery
- the slope of the curve is equal to negative daily carry
- the basis converges to zero as time approaches delivery

**Chart 1.1   Basis of Cheapest to Deliver if Known
                   and Carry is Positive**

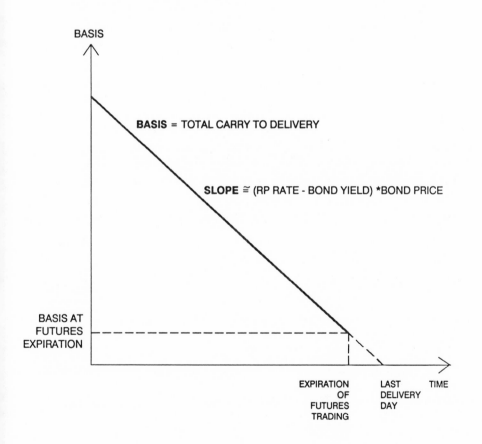

In Chart 1.1, the basis relationship is drawn for a setting in which carry is positive. Also note that the basis is represented by a solid line only until the last trading day is reached. After trading in the futures contract has expired, the futures price is fixed while the bond's price is free to change. Both of these are important features of the bond basis market and we discuss them further in Chapters 2 and 3.

Implied Repo Rate

The implied repo rate is the theoretical return you would obtain if you bought the cash bond, sold futures short against it, and then delivered the cash bond into the futures. The formula for the implied repo rate is:

IRR = [(Invoice Price/Purchase Price − 1) × 360]/n

where n is the number of days to delivery, and the invoice and purchase prices include accrued interest. (If a coupon payment falls within the period, the calculation is slightly different.)

Consider the calculation of the implied repo rate on February 19, 1988 for the 12s of 8/15/13-08, assuming delivery on the last possible date for delivery into the March 1988 contract (3/31/88). On February 19, futures settled at 93-22/32nds. There were 38 days left until the last delivery date from the cash settlement date (2/22/88). The cash price was quoted at 131-30/32nds and accrued interest on $100 face value of the bonds from the last coupon payment date (2/15/88) to settlement (2/22/88) was $0.23. At delivery accrued interest would be $1.48.

To calculate the implied repo rate for $100,000 par value of the bond, obtain the purchase price:

Purchase Price = Quoted Price + Accrued Interest
               = $131.93750 + $.23
               = $132.17

(See Table 1.1 column 10.)

Given delivery on March 31 and a futures price of 93-22/32nds, the invoice price would be:

Invoice Price = Converted Futures Price + Accrued Interest
= $93.68750 × 1.3976 + $1.48
= $130.93765 + $1.48
= $132.42

With these numbers, the implied repo rate is:

IRR = [($132.42/$132.17) − 1] × 360/38
= 1.79%

(See Table 1.1 column 16.)

Important Points The implied repo rate is a theoretical return. The calculation assumes that you are short C futures for each $100,000 bonds held long and that any coupon payments can be invested at the yield on the bonds. Even then, you can only approximate the return because of variation margin payments on the futures contract. As prices rise, you lose money on your short futures position, and this must be paid through to whoever is long the futures. As prices fall, of course, you collect variation margin payments. Notice, however, that you are paying out variation margin when yields are high and receiving variation margin when yields are low. The overall effect may not be very large, but it is enough to drive a wedge between the theoretical and actual return.

Terminology varies, and occasionally you will find the implied repo rate called the "breakeven" repo rate. For example, on Telerate page 8016 (at this writing), the next to last column shows implied repo rates labeled "BE REPO."

Buying and Selling the Basis

Basis trading is the simultaneous trading of cash bonds and bond futures to take advantage of expected changes in the basis. To "buy the basis" or to "go long the basis" is to buy cash bonds and to sell a number of futures contracts equal to the conversion factor for every $100,000 par value cash bond. To "sell the basis" or to "go short the basis" is just the opposite: selling or shorting the cash bond and buying the futures contracts.

There are two reasons for using the bond's conversion factor as the number of futures to buy or sell in a basis trade:

1. Cash and futures prices do not move one-for-one, so that a cash/futures position in which cash and futures were combined in equal par values would be exposed to changes in the level of bond and futures prices. **A bond's conversion factor approximates the number of futures required for each $100,000 par value of the cash bonds to remove the directional bias.**

2. A bond's conversion factor defines its basis. If futures and bonds are combined in a ratio equal to the bond's conversion factor, a change in the bond's basis of any given amount will yield the same profit regardless of whether the change in the basis comes from a change in the price of the bond or a change in the futures price, and regardless of whether bond and futures prices generally rise or generally fall. Combining cash and futures in ratios other than the bond's conversion factor will produce different payoffs for the same change in the basis if the basis change accompanies price increases or price decreases. (Chapter 4 delves further into this aspect of basis trading.)

There are two sources of profit in a basis position:

- change in the basis
- carry

A long basis position profits from an increase in the basis. Further, if net carry on the bond is positive, the long basis position picks up the carry as well. Conversely, a short basis position profits from a decrease in the basis but loses the carry if carry is positive.

The profit/loss characteristics of basis trades are best illustrated with an example of each.

Buying the Basis

Suppose that on January 20, 1988, futures are trading at 90-06/32nds. At the same time, 7-1/4s of 2016 are trading at 83-18/32nds for a basis of 28/32nds. You think that 28/32nds is a narrow basis at this time in the delivery cycle and that it is likely to widen out. Table 1.1 shows that the 7-1/4s had a conversion factor of .9167. Your opening trade would be:

On 1/20/88 (settle 1/21/88)

> Buy $1MM of 7-1/4s of 5/16 at 83-18/32nds
> Sell 9 March 1988 futures at 90-06/32nds
> Basis = 28/32nds

By February 5, your views have been borne out, and you want to unwind the position. Your closing trade would be:

On 2/05/88 (settle 2/06/88)

> Sell $1MM of 7-1/4s of 5/16 at 87-11/32nds
> Buy 9 March 1988 futures at 94-04/32nds
> Basis = 34/32nds

Profit/Loss

> Buy 1MM 7-1/4% at 83.18
> Sell 1MM 7-1/4% at 87.11
> $121/32nds \times \$312.50 = \$37,812.50$

Sell 9 March 1988 futures at 90-06/32nds
Buy 9 March 1988 futures at 94-04/32nds
$\qquad$ 126/32nds × 9 × $31.25 = ($35,437.50)

Coupon interest earned (16 days)
$\qquad$ $1,000,000 × .0725 × 16/365 = $3,178.08

RP interest paid (16 days)
—calculated for purchase price + accrued interest
$\qquad$ $848,970.00 × .0665 × 16/360 = ($2,509.18)

Summary P/L

7-1/4s of 16	$37,812.50
March 1988 futures	(35,437.50)
Coupon interest	3,178.08
RP interest	(2,509.18)
Total	$ 3,043.90

Alternative Summary P/L

The summary P/L can be reduced further still into the two fundamental sources of profit to a basis trade: change in the basis and carry. For this particular trade, these would be:

Change in the basis	$2,375.00
Carry	668.90
Total	$3,043.90

where the change in the basis is the sum of what you made on the 7-1/4s and lost on the March 1988 futures, while carry is the combined value of coupon interest received and RP interest paid.

Selling the Basis

In contrast to the basis of the 7-1/4s, you believe that the basis of the 12s of 2013 on January 20 is too wide and will narrow substantially over the next few days. From Table 1.1, we know that the conversion factor of the 12s was 1.3976. Your opening trade is:

On 1/20/88 (settle 1/21/88)

Sell $1MM of 12s of 8/13-08 at 128-06/32nds

Buy 14 March 1988 futures at 90-06/32nds

Basis = 69/32nds

By February 5, the basis has narrowed enough to close out the position. Your closing trade is:

On 2/05/88 (settle 2/06/88)

Buy $1MM of 12s of 8/13-08 at 132-24/32nds

Sell 14 March '88 futures at 94-04/32nds

Basis = 38/32nds

Profit/Loss

Sell 1MM 12s at 128-06/32nds

Buy 1MM 12s at 132-24/32nds

146/32nds × $312.50 = ($45,625.00)

Buy 14 March 1988 futures at 90-06/32nds

Sell 14 March 1988 futures at 94-04/32nds

126/32nds × 14 × $31.25 = $55,125.00

Coupon interest paid (16 days)

$1,000,000 × .12 × 16/365 = ($5,260.27)

Reverse RP interest earned (16 days)

—calculated for sale price + accrued interest

$1,333,723 × .0665 × 16/360 = $3,941.89

Summary P/L

12s of 13-08	(45,625.00)
March 1988 futures	55,125.00
Coupon interest	(5,260.27)
RP interest	3,941.89
Total	$ 8,181.62

Alternative Summary P/L

Change in the basis	$9500.00
Carry	($1318.38)
Total	$ 8181.62

RP Versus Reverse RP Rates

RP stands for repurchase, or "repo." Standard industry practice in the U.S. Treasury bond market is to finance long securities positions through the use of repurchase agreements. Formally, at least, a *repurchase agreement* is an arrangement in which a bond is sold today at one price and bought back at a later date, often the next day, at a predetermined price that is usually higher. The effect of this transaction is to finance the position, and the difference in the two prices is the cost of financing the position. When the cost is expressed in annual percentage terms, the resulting figure is the RP, or *repo*, rate. Note that because the repurchase price is set in advance, the RP rate is a comparatively risk-free short-term rate of return.

In a reverse repo, a bond is "reversed in" at one price and sold back later at a predetermined price that is usually higher. The effect of this transaction is to lend money at a comparatively risk-free short-term rate.

Repo transactions can be either overnight or for a set term. If the repurchase is set for the next day, the repo is overnight. If the repurchase is set for any longer period of time, the repo is *term*.

Under normal circumstances, the reverse repo rate trades 25 to 75 basis points below the repo rate. That is, the rate at which you can finance long positions in Treasuries is 25 to 75 basis points higher than the rate at which you can invest money short term.

The difference can have a substantial effect on the profitability of basis trades. Suppose, for example, that the reverse repo rate in the example of selling the basis had been 6.10 percent (55 basis points) lower than the repo rate. At this rate, our profit from selling the basis would have been $7,855.60, or $326.02 less. Had the bond been "on special" (discussed in Chapter 4) and the reverse repo rate had been 3 percent, the total profit on the trade would have been $6,018.03—more than $2,000 less than with the RP rate at 6.65 percent.

An Idealized Strategy for Trading the Bond Basis

The smooth convergence of the bond basis shown in Chart 1.1 is a radical simplification of how the bond basis behaves. For a variety of reasons, one of which is uncertainty about short-term financing costs, a bond's basis follows a rockier road.

The basis illustrated in Chart 1.2 follows a rocky road, indeed, rockier for that matter than it has really been recently. Over the past couple of years, short-term financing rates have stabilized considerably and the costs of trading the basis have become quite low for large traders who are close to the market. As a result, the road has become smoother, and the strategy now is profitable only for a highly efficient set of traders—most notably the primary government securities dealers.

The purpose of Chart 1.2, however, is to illustrate an idealized strategy for trading the bond basis. Consider the following rules for trading. You recognize that the basis can bounce around from day to

Chart 1.2 A Strategy for Trading the Bond Basis

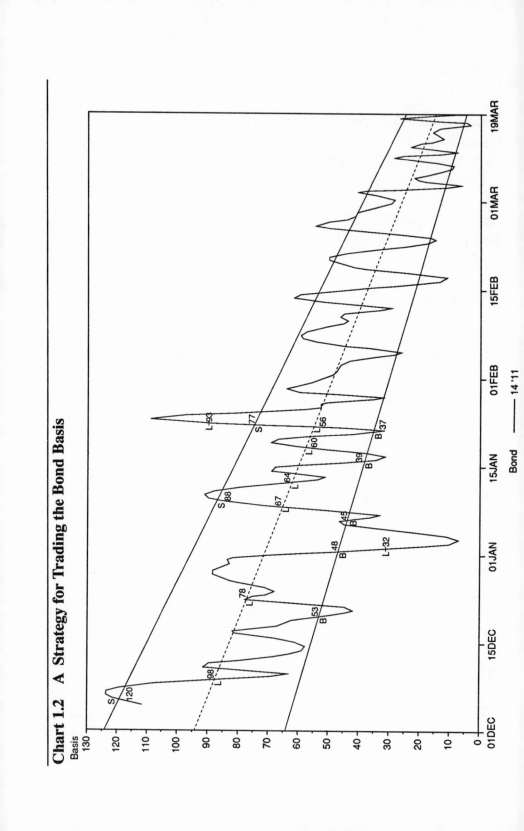

Basis

— Bond   — 14 '11

day, but you also believe strongly that the basis should not trade at implied repo rates higher than 4 percent or lower than 1 percent. In Chart 1.2, solid diagonal lines represent these upper and lower bounds. You decide to sell the basis whenever it trades above the upper bound and liquidate the position whenever it trades at or below the mid-point of the range. Similarly, you buy the basis whenever it trades below the lower bound and liquidate the position whenever it trades at or above the mid-point of the range.

As it stands, such a strategy sounds like a sure winner, but any realistic trading strategy must allow for the possibility that the entire financing structure may change. A sharp increase in short-term financing costs would shift the trading bounds up. A sharp steepening of the yield curve would shift the trading bounds down. In either case, you should have a rule for bailing out. For this example, assume that you liquidate the trade if it moves 16/32nds against you.

Armed with such a rule, the resulting set of trades would be:

1	Sell at 120/32nds, liquidate at 98/32nds, net 22/32nds
2	Buy at 53/32nds, liquidate at 78/32nds, net 25/32nds
3	Buy at 48/32nds, liquidate at 32/32nds, net −16/32nds
4	Buy at 45/32nds, liquidate at 67/32nds, net 22/32nds
5	Sell at 88/32nds, liquidate at 64/32nds, net 24/32nds
6	Buy at 39/32nds, liquidate at 60/32nds, net 21/32nds
7	Buy at 37/32nds, liquidate at 56/32nds, net 19/32nds
8	Sell at 77/32nds, liquidate at 93/32nds, net −16/32nds

The net income from these trades amounts to 101/32nds not counting carry, which would have been more or less a wash. Note that the third and eighth trades were both half-point losers.

Why stop at the eighth trade? One of the key ingredients of any trading strategy is an expected profit objective. Notice that the range of possible outcomes narrows as the expiration of trading in the futures contract approaches. As the range narrows, the expected profit from each trade gets smaller relative to the cost of doing the trade, which are roughly the same no matter when the trade is done. Thus, in this ideal-ized example, we stop trading when the futures has about two months remaining to expiration. At this point, the expected profit from a trade is too small to warrant the trading costs and risks.

In the real world of basis trading, as in the real world of almost any-thing, things are just more complicated. The purpose of this book, however, is to explain those complications and to make trading the bond basis both understandable and accessible.

Chapter 2

What Drives the Basis?

From a strict carry standpoint, futures prices are too low. Those who buy bonds and sell futures cannot make enough in carry to compensate for the lower futures price. Those who sell bonds and buy futures seem to more than make up for the carry they lose. In a nutshell, basis tends to exceed carry and has done so persistently for the past several years.

The players in the bond market are some of the brightest people in the financial world, and so we cannot chalk up the difference to ignorance or stupidity. Instead, we should expect to find that those who sell the futures are getting something other than carry in return. On the other side of the trade, of course, those who buy the futures must be giving up whatever the shorts expect to gain. For those who are long futures, then, the difference between basis and carry is what they receive for whatever it is they are giving up.

What accounts for the difference? The answer lies in the short's right to choose which bond to deliver and when to deliver it.

The Short's Alternatives

If there were only one bond that could be delivered into the futures contract and only one day on which delivery could be made, understanding the bond basis would be a breeze. Competitive forces would cause the bond basis for the one deliverable bond to be equal to net carry, and the relationship between the basis and the time to delivery would look like the graph in Chart 1.1.

As it is, there were 31 bonds that were eligible on February 19 for delivery into the Board of Trade's bond futures contract, each with its own basis, carry, conversion factor, yield, and implied repo rate. Further, the ongoing funding of the U.S. budget deficit periodically introduces bonds with new coupons and maturities into the eligible set of deliverable bonds. A basis trade can involve any one of these eligible issues.

Moreover, the delivery window is a full month long. Delivery can be made on any business day of the contract month. This includes seven business days after the futures have stopped trading.

Under the rules that govern the Chicago Board of Trade's bond futures contract, the one who is short the contract is the one who decides which bond to deliver and when to deliver it. The short strives, of course, to pick both the bond and the delivery day that work to his or her best advantage.

Chapter 3 describes how the short's ability to shift out of one bond into another is worth something, as is the short's right to deliver early in the delivery month rather than later. The value of these rights is what accounts for the difference between basis and carry. Moreover, changes in the values of these rights account for changes in the difference between basis and carry.

Search for the Cheapest Bond to Deliver

The search for the best bond to deliver is, in the language of futures, the search for the "cheapest to deliver." Because the cheapest to deliver can shift from one bond to another, many of the interesting questions for basis traders revolve around this search.

The key concepts covered in this section are:

- cheapest to deliver
- shifts in the cheapest to deliver
- the likelihood of a shift in the cheapest to deliver

- the cost of a shift in the cheapest to deliver
- optimal timing of deliveries

Cheapest to Deliver

The cheapest bond to deliver is the bond that maximizes the return to buying the cash bond, carrying the bond to delivery, and delivering the bond into the bond futures contract.

A rough-and-ready way to find the cheapest to deliver is to compare a bond's basis with its total carry to delivery. The difference is called the *premium*. As shown in Table 2.1, the 10-3/8s of 2012 had a basis of 19/32nds on February 19 and estimated general carry to delivery of 7.955/32nds. The 10-3/8s were trading about "11/32nds over carry." By contrast, the 8-3/4s of 2017 had a basis of 39/32nds, estimated carry to delivery of 5.609/32nds, and so were trading 33.4/32nds over carry.

The net cost of buying the 10-3/8s and delivering them into the futures contract would be 11/32nds while the net cost of doing the same thing with the 8-3/4s would be 33.4/32nds. By this measure, then, the 10-3/8s would the cheaper bond to deliver.

The chief drawback to this approach is that it can give incorrect rankings when the premiums for two bonds are very close to one another. To be precise, basis net of carry should be compared with the total purchase price of the bond, inclusive of accrued interest, which depends in turn on its coupon and maturity for any given level of yields.

The most precise way to find the cheapest to deliver is to find the bond with the highest implied repo rate. The implied repo rate is the rate of return to buying the cash bond and delivering it into the futures contract. As a result, the implied repo rate takes into account the bond's purchase price.

Table 2.1 shows the implied repo rates for all eligible bonds as of February 19, 1988. The implied repo rates for the last delivery day range from –9.41 percent for the 9-3/8s of 2006 to 3.96 percent for the 10-3/8s of 2012-07. Thus, the cheapest bond to deliver on February 19

Table 2.1 Choosing the Cheapest Bond to Deliver and the Best Time to Deliver It

BEST TIME TO DELIVER →

COUPON	MATURITY	CASH PRICE 2/19/88	CONVERSION FACTOR	BASIS	CARRY DOLLARS PER DAY	CARRY 32nds PER DAY	TOTAL CARRY 32nds TO LAST DELIVERY DAY	IMPLIED RP RATE TO FIRST DELIVERY DAY	IMPLIED RP RATE TO FUTURES EXPIRATION DAY	IMPLIED RP RATE TO LAST DELIVERY DAY
10.750	06/15/03	118.01	1.2378	66	71.90	0.230	8.743	-88.06	-12.43	-7.41
11.125	08/15/03	121.12	1.2723	70	61.03	0.259	9.863	-71.52	-13.20	-7.93
11.875	11/15/03	127.21	1.3408	65	84.46	0.270	10.270	-81.19	-10.40	-5.82
12.375	05/15/04	132.12	1.3910	66	89.23	0.286	10.850	-59.16	-9.81	-5.38
13.750	08/15/04	145.00	1.5175	91	109.41	0.350	13.304	-78.31	-14.84	-6.12
11.625	11/15/04	126.08	1.3289	56	80.32	0.257	9.768	-51.95	-7.91	-3.94
12.000	05/15/05	130.04	1.3682	62	83.27	0.266	10.128	-56.64	-8.20	-4.92
10.750	08/15/05	118.26	1.2546	41	75.47	0.242	9.178	-39.19	-4.36	-1.22
9.375	02/15/06	107.26	1.1289	66	58.07	0.186	7.081	-76.81	-14.99	-9.41
8.375	08/15/08-03	97.30	1.0325	39	48.87	0.156	5.043	-46.86	-8.63	-3.22
8.750	11/15/08-03	101.08	1.0680	44	48.86	0.157	5.063	-51.56	-8.19	-4.28
9.125	05/15/09-04	104.10	1.1005	39	53.41	0.171	6.495	-62.54	-5.63	-2.30
10.375	11/15/09-04	114.27	1.2155	31	67.67	0.217	8.229	-28.27	-1.50	0.91
11.750	02/15/10-05	127.12	1.3425	51	87.09	0.279	10.591	-47.33	-6.48	-2.79
10.000	05/15/10-05	111.30	1.1841	32	62.93	0.201	7.652	-30.73	-2.25	0.32
12.750	11/15/10-05	136.27	1.4433	52	91.09	0.291	11.076	-43.14	-5.41	-2.01
13.875	05/15/11-06	147.25	1.5554	66	101.23	0.324	12.309	-52.13	-7.64	-3.85
14.000	11/15/11-06	149.14	1.5743	82	101.54	0.325	12.347	-48.11	-6.75	-3.02
10.375	11/15/12-07	116.02	1.2326	19	65.42	0.209	7.955	-13.47	2.52	3.96
12.000	08/15/13-08	131.30	1.3976	32	85.53	0.274	10.400	-25.09	-0.44	1.79
13.250	05/15/14-09	144.19	1.5366	40	90.26	0.289	10.975	-29.46	-1.75	0.76
12.500	08/15/14-09	137.23	1.4500	42	88.57	0.283	10.770	-33.79	-2.85	-0.06
11.750	11/15/14-09	130.16	1.3820	33	75.84	0.243	9.222	-25.60	-0.84	1.41
11.250	02/15/15	128.18	1.3561	48	71.18	0.228	8.656	-44.25	-5.97	-2.51
10.625	08/15/15	122.17	1.2892	56	65.18	0.209	7.925	-55.60	-9.15	-4.96
9.875	11/15/15	114.09	1.2073	38	55.23	0.177	6.716	-38.78	-4.12	-1.17
9.250	02/15/16	107.24	1.1383	35	54.75	0.175	6.658	-37.64	-4.26	-1.25
7.250	05/15/16	86.24	0.9167	28	35.29	0.113	4.291	-35.90	-4.07	-1.19
7.500	11/15/16	89.15	0.9442	32	37.01	0.118	4.500	-41.54	-5.60	-2.36
8.750	05/15/17	102.25	1.0641	39	48.13	0.148	5.609	-43.77	-6.13	-2.74
8.875	08/15/17	104.23	1.0681	59	50.06	0.160	6.086	-70.82	-13.44	-8.28

CHEAPEST TO DELIVER →

Source: Table 1.1

would have been the 10-3/8s. Note that the implied repo rate for the 8-3/4s of 2017 was −2.74 percent.

You should note, too, that the implied repo rate for each bond is higher for the last delivery date than for either of the earlier dates. Thus, the implied repo rate is not only a guide to the cheapest to deliver. It is a guide to the optimal delivery date as well. In this case, the best delivery date is the last possible delivery date.

Shifts in the Cheapest to Deliver

The cheapest bond to deliver changes from time to time, usually because the level of yields or the slope of the yield curve changes, and occasionally because a new bond is added to the eligible set through the Treasury's funding of the budget deficit. On any given day, of course, the implied repo rate can pinpoint accurately the cheapest bond to deliver but gives no insight into why the cheapest to deliver changes from one bond to another.

This section describes the forces that cause the cheapest bond to deliver to change. The choice of the cheapest to deliver can be characterized in terms of duration and yield.

The general rules of thumb for yield and duration are:

Duration For bonds trading at the same yield *below* 8 percent, the bond with the lowest duration will be the cheapest to deliver. For bonds trading at the same yield *above* 8 percent, the bond with the longest duration will be the cheapest to deliver.

Yield For bonds with the same duration, the bond with the highest yield will be the cheapest bond to deliver.

Duration The important thing to know about a bond's duration is that it represents the percentage change in the price of the bond for a given change in the bond's yield. For the same change in yields, then, the prices of high-duration bonds change relatively more than the prices of low-duration bonds.

Why is this important? The Board of Trade's conversion factors are the approximate prices at which bonds eligible for delivery would yield 8 percent. As a result, the conversion factors are neutral at 8 percent. If all deliverable bonds were trading at 8 percent (their respective converted prices), their prices divided by conversion factor would all equal 100. Anyone making delivery would be indifferent between any two eligible bonds.

Chart 2.1 shows a simple two-bond example in a graph of the converted prices of a high-duration bond against the converted prices of a low-duration bond. Note that if both bonds yield exactly 8 percent (and ignoring the rounding to the nearest calendar quarter that is used in determining conversion factors), both bonds will have converted prices of 100. In such a case, the short would be indifferent between the two bonds. Each is just as cheap to deliver as the other.

Rule of Thumb

At yields above and below 8 percent, however, duration plays a factor. Consider yields below 8 percent. As yields fall from 8 percent, the prices of both bonds rise. But the price of the low-duration bond rises relatively less than the price of the high-duration bond. Thus, as yields fall below 8 percent, the low-duration bond becomes the cheaper to deliver.

In contrast, as yields rise above 8 percent, the price of the high-duration bond falls relatively more than the price of the low-duration bond. As a result, the high-duration bond becomes the cheaper bond to deliver at yields above 8 percent.

Relative Yield   Bonds do not all trade at identical yields. As shown in Table 1.1, the yields on deliverable bonds for February 19, 1988, ranged from 8.438 percent to 8.674 percent. Bond yields depend on any number of things, including the size of the coupon, whether the bond is callable, whether the bond is readily available for trading, and so forth. Whatever the reasons, though, it is possible to find bonds with roughly the same duration trading at substantially different yields.

Chart 2.1 Finding the Cheapest Bond to Deliver

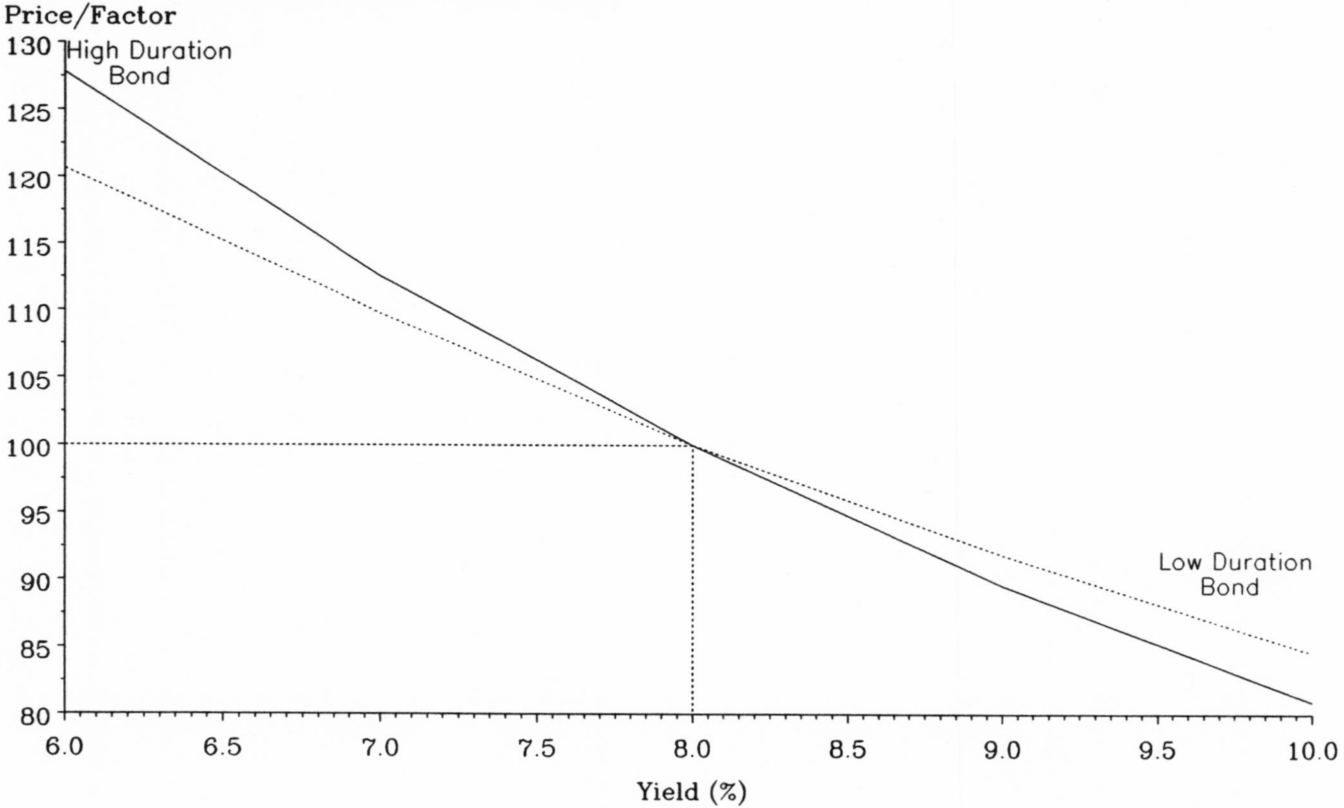

Price/Factor

High Duration Bond: 7 1/4's of '16. Low Duration Bond: 14's of '11.

Rule of Thumb

For bonds with the same duration, the bond with the highest yield will be the cheapest to deliver.

Experience Over the Past Several Deliveries   These rules of thumb can be checked against actual experience with deliveries into the Board of Trade's bond contract.

To illustrate the importance of yield and duration in determining the cheapest bond to deliver, Chart 2.2 shows a graph of the level of yields (Chart 2.2A) against the relative duration and relative yield of the most heavily delivered bond (Chart 2.2B) in each of the delivery cycles from 1983 to date. For this illustration, relative duration is measured as:

$$(D - D_l)/(D_h - D_l)$$

where

   D is the duration of the delivered bond
   D_l is the duration of the bond with the lowest duration in the eligible set
   D_h is the duration of the highest duration bond in the eligible set.

Relative yield is measured similarly.

Chart 2.2 shows a strong relationship between the level of yields and the yield and duration characteristics of the most heavily-delivered bonds, which we can assume with considerable confidence were the cheapest to deliver at the time. When yields are high, the cheapest bond to deliver has a relatively high duration and a relatively low yield. On the other hand, when yields have been around 8 percent, it has been the relative yield of the bond that has been the deciding factor.

The crossover point seems to be around 9 percent. Why not 8 percent?

Not all the eligible bonds trade at the same yield. The low-duration bonds tend to trade at slightly higher yields than do the high-duration

Chart 2.2A   Average Deliverable Bond Yield (R) vs. Delivery Date

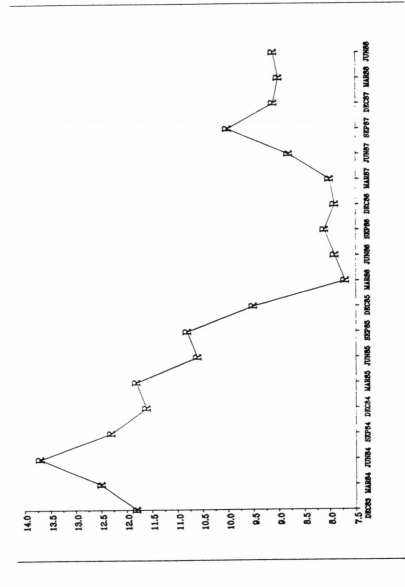

Chart 2.2B   Relative Yield (Y) and Duration (D) of Most Heavily Delivered Bond vs. Delivery Date

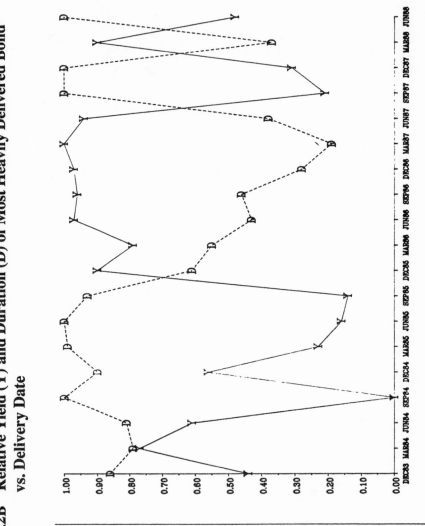

Source: DCNYF Research Database

bonds. As a result, yields have to rise enough above 8 percent for the relative price effect on the high-duration bond to overcome the yield advantage of the low-duration bond. Given the range of yield spreads at which bonds traded over the past several years, the crossover point seems to have been around 9 percent.

The Likelihood of a Shift in the Cheapest to Deliver

Because a shift in the deliverable bond can have a substantial effect on the basis of each eligible bond, we find it worthwhile to assess the likelihood of a shift in the cheapest to deliver. Our approach is illustrated in Table 2.2. The bonds included in Table 2.2 are a subset of those in Table 1.1; the bonds which are illiquid have been excluded.

The construction of Table 2.2 begins in a fairly straightforward way, with whatever the current distribution of yields on eligible bonds happens to be. Then it shows what the cheapest to deliver would be at the expiration of futures trading if yields

- stayed unchanged
- increased by 50, 100, or 200 basis points
- fell by 50, 100, or 200 basis points

These questions are answered by first calculating what each bond's price would be at the expiration of futures trading and then dividing each bond's price by its own conversion factor. This puts all the bond prices on an equal footing. The lowest of the converted bond prices is what the cheapest to deliver would be if the assumed set of yields were to prevail.

Once we have identified the most likely candidate for cheapest to deliver at any given level of yields, we calculate a hypothetical futures price by assuming that the basis of the cheapest to deliver would be 6/32nds. Any other assumption would do for the purposes of ranking the bonds, but 6/32nds seems like a reasonable number given the range of bases observed at the expiration of futures trading. From this

Table 2.2   Assessing Shifts in the Cheapest to Deliver Bond*
(Basis on Last Trading Day Given Yields on February 19, 1987)

ISSUE		CURRENT MARKET (2/19/88)			BASIS PROJECTIONS — CHANGE IN YIELDS (IN BASIS POINTS)														
					-200		-100		-50		0		+50		+100		+200	
COUPON	MATURITY	PRICE	YIELD	BASIS	YIELD	BASIS	YIELD	BASIS	YIELD	BASIS	YIELD	BASIS	YIELD	BASIS	YIELD	BASIS	YIELD	BASIS
10.750	08/15/05	118.26	8.644	41	6.644	19	7.644	9	8.144	17	8.644	27	9.144	50	9.644	83	10.644	133
9.375	02/15/06	107.26	8.518	66	6.518	86	7.518	55	8.018	53	8.518	54	9.018	67	9.518	90	10.518	124
8.750	11/15/08-03	101.08	8.601	44	6.601	20	7.601	16	8.101	25	8.601	34	9.101	53	9.601	82	10.601	123
9.125	05/15/09-04	104.10	8.624	39	6.624	17	7.624	11	8.124	19	8.624	28	9.124	48	9.624	77	10.624	119
12.750	11/15/10-05	136.27	8.646	52	6.646	6	7.646	6	8.146	21	8.646	36	9.146	66	9.646	108	10.646	171
14.000	11/15/11-06	149.14	8.627	62	6.627	26	7.627	18	8.127	30	8.627	44	9.127	75	9.627	119	10.627	186
10.375	11/15/12-07	116.02	8.659	19	6.659	47	7.659	9	8.159	6	8.659	6	9.159	20	9.659	47	10.659	86
12.000	08/15/13-08	131.30	8.646	32	6.646	58	7.646	17	8.146	15	8.646	16	9.146	34	9.646	65	10.646	112
13.250	05/15/14-09	144.19	8.630	40	6.630	73	7.630	26	8.130	23	8.630	24	9.130	43	9.630	77	10.630	127
12.500	08/15/14-09	137.23	8.615	42	6.615	88	7.615	34	8.115	28	8.615	26	9.115	41	9.615	71	10.615	116
11.750	11/15/14-09	130.16	8.618	33	6.618	91	7.618	32	8.118	23	8.618	18	9.118	31	9.618	57	10.618	97
11.250	02/15/15	128.18	8.528	48	6.528	213	7.528	92	8.028	59	8.528	34	9.028	30	9.528	42	10.528	61
10.625	08/15/15	122.17	8.494	56	6.494	232	7.494	106	7.994	70	8.494	42	8.994	35	9.494	44	10.494	58
9.875	11/15/15	114.09	8.522	38	6.522	212	7.522	88	8.022	53	8.522	26	9.022	18	9.522	25	10.522	37
9.250	02/15/16	107.24	8.519	35	6.519	211	7.519	88	8.019	51	8.519	24	9.019	14	9.519	20	10.519	29
7.250	05/15/16	86.24	8.492	28	6.492	205	7.492	85	7.992	48	8.492	19	8.992	6	9.492	6	10.492	6
7.500	11/15/16	89.15	8.482	32	6.482	216	7.482	92	7.982	53	8.482	23	8.982	10	9.482	10	10.482	10
8.750	05/15/17	102.25	8.489	39	6.489	231	7.489	99	7.989	59	8.489	28	8.989	16	9.489	18	10.489	23
8.875	08/15/17	104.23	8.438	59	6.438	263	7.438	123	7.938	81	8.438	48	8.938	33	9.438	35	10.438	37
Bond futures price		93.22			112.22		103.03		98.13		93.32		89.16		84.32		77.01	

* This report is available daily from DCNYF.
Source: DCNYF Research

hypothetical futures price, simply calculate bases for the eligible bonds in the usual way.

The results of this exercise are instructive. On February 19, yields were trading at around 8.5 percent. The cheapest to deliver bond was the 10-3/8s of 11/12-07, which had a basis of 19/32nds. The cheapness of the 10-3/8s is confirmed by the basis projections in the column that corresponds to no change in yields. Given the construction the table, the hallmark of the cheapest to deliver is a projected basis of 6/32nds. The center column, which corresponds to no change in the level of yields, shows that the bond with this distinction is the 10-3/8s of 11/12-07.

How secure is its position as the cheapest to deliver? Consider what happens to the projected basis of the 10-3/8s of 11/12-07 as yields rise or fall. If yields fall by 50 basis points, the 10-3/8s stays cheapest to deliver. If yields fall by 100 basis points, however, the cheapest to deliver bond shifts to the 12-3/4s of 11/10-05. The 12-3/4s would also be the cheapest to deliver if yields were to fall by another 100 basis points.

A rise in yields also prompts a shift in the cheapest to deliver. A 50-basis-point increase in yields which puts yields in the area of 9 percent prompts a shift to the 7-1/4s of 5/16 as the cheapest to deliver. Further increases in yields only cement the cheapness of the 7-1/4s.

How likely is a shift in the deliverable bond? Table 2.2 cannot answer this question. The answer depends on how volatile long-term bond yields are and how much time remains to the expiration of futures trading. There is about a month between February 19 and the last day of trading in the March futures contract. Yields were also fairly volatile, so that the probability of yields increasing by 50 basis points was quite high. Yields were not so volatile, however, that a decrease in yields of 100 basis points was much to worry about. Thus, if there were to be a change in the cheapest to deliver, the most likely shift was toward the 7-1/4s because of an increase in yields, and the chance of this happening was large enough to deserve consideration.

Cost of a Shift in the Cheapest to Deliver

How costly is a shift in the deliverable bond? Table 2.2 is especially good at answering this question. Suppose you decide to short the basis of the 10-3/8s of 11/12-07 on February 19th which settles on February 22nd. The basis is 19/32nds, and Table 1.1 shows that there are 29 days left to expiration of the March futures and that daily carry on the 10-3/8s of 11/12-07 is about .21/32nds. The cost of shorting the 10-3/8s of 11/12-07 between February 19 and the last day of futures trading would then be just over 6/32nds. Thus, if you sell the 10-3/8s basis on the 19th for 19/32nds (a coincidence, to be sure), buy it back for 6/32nds on the last day of trading, our gross income would be 13/32nds. Of this, you have to give up the carry of 6/32nds, so that your net income would be 7/32nds.

The trade can lose money, however, if yields either rise or fall substantially. For example, if yields rise 50 basis points, the projected basis of the 10-3/8s on the last day of futures trading is 20/32nds. Remember that several assumptions went into this calculation, and that the actual basis of the 10-3/8s might well be several 32nds higher or lower than 20/32nds. Even so, the direction of the change is clear. If yields rise and the 7-1/4s become the cheapest to deliver by the close of futures trading, the only effect this can have on the basis of the 10-3/8s is to increase it.

If the basis of the 10-3/8s settles at 20/32nds on the last day of futures trading, the gross income on the trade would be a loss of 1/32nd compounded by the 6/32nds that would be given up in carry. The total profit on the trade would be a loss of 7/32nds rather than a gain of 7/32nds.

You are not locked into a trade, and there is nothing to prevent you from swapping out of the 10-3/8s when they become relatively expensive to deliver and into the 7-1/4s as they become the cheapest to deliver. By monitoring a trade and swapping into whatever happens to be the current cheapest to deliver, you can limit potential losses from shorting the basis. This is not true, however, of basis sales involving bonds other than the cheapest to deliver.

A decrease in yields starting from the levels set on February 19 would not have as great an effect on the profitability of the trade. Yields would have to fall farther to knock the 10-3/8s out of their position as cheapest to deliver. For example, even if yields were to fall 100 basis points, the 12-3/4s would become the cheapest to deliver bond but by a fairly narrow margin. The basis of the 10-3/8s would still be only 9/32nds, compared with the assumed 6/32nds of the cheapest to deliver. Thus, if yields were to fall 100 basis points, the trade would still be profitable. The gross income would be 10/32nds from selling the basis at 19/32nds and buying it back at 9/32nds. Given the carry costs of 6/32nds, the net profit would be 4/32nds.

Optimal Timing of Deliveries
Delivery into the Chicago Board of Trade bond futures contract can take place on any business day during the contract month. Since the futures contract stops trading on the 8th business day before the end of the contract month, delivery can take place up to one week after the invoice price is determined. When should the short make delivery?

Positively-Sloped Yield Curve   If long-term yields are higher than short-term yields, the short's decision about when to make delivery is fairly simple. There are two forces working on the decision, both tending to make the short choose the last possible delivery day.

First, the short who makes delivery gives up any remaining value in the options to change the deliverable bond. The value of these options is the difference between the basis of the cheapest to deliver and its remaining carry to the last delivery day. This difference, or premium, can amount to several 32nds, even for the cheapest to deliver.

Second, if the yield curve has a positive slope, carry for someone who is long bonds and short futures is positive. Every day that goes by is money in the bank. The implied repo rate confirms this. Table 2.1 shows implied repo rates for three different delivery days including the first possible day, the last day of futures trading, and the last possible day. The implied repo rate is highest for the last possible delivery day.

Only a "wild card" or "switch" opportunity will cause the short to give up the current basis and make delivery early. (See Chapter 3 for details.)

Negatively-Sloped Yield Curve   The short's problem is somewhat more complex if carry is negative. Every day that goes by is a drain, because what is being made in the form of coupon income is not enough to make up for the cost of financing the position in the RP market.

The way to avoid the negative carry, of course, is to make delivery early. The chief problem with early delivery is that the short must give up the remaining value of the various delivery options.

Early delivery is worthwhile only under fairly extreme circumstances. It is profitable if the value of negative carry dominates the value of the delivery options. Using the past as a guide, we find that the RP rate has had to be significantly higher than long-term bond yields to justify making early delivery.

Compare the delivery pattern for the March 1988 futures contract with the delivery pattern for the June 1981 futures contract (see Tables 2.3 and 2.4). In March 1988, the yield curve was positively sloped, and all but a few stray deliveries were made on the last possible delivery day of the contract month. In June 1981, however, the yield curve sloped steeply downward. The pattern of deliveries suggests powerful offsetting forces at work on delivery decisions. A substantial number of bonds was delivered early in the month. Just as interesting were the deliveries that were strung out through the month and the big chunk of deliveries that was made on the last day. Those who made delivery after the first delivery day were paying substantial negative carry for the privilege of waiting.

Table 2.3 Bond Deliveries, March 1988

DATE (YYMMDD)	COUPON	MATURITY	NUMBER DELIVERED	FACTOR
880331	10.375	11/15/12-07	7137	1.2326
880331	7.250	5/15/16	50	0.9167
880330	10.375	11/15/12-07	110	1.2326
880330	7.250	5/15/16	1	0.9167
880329	7.250	5/15/16	200	0.9167
880328	7.250	5/15/16	2	0.9167
880318	12.000	8/15/13-08	100	1.3976
880318	7.250	5/15/16	50	0.9167
880318	10.375	11/15/12-07	50	1.2326
880309	7.250	5/15/16	10	0.9167
880301	13.250	5/15/14-09	3	1.5299

Total Deliveries, Average conversion Factor = 7713   1.2220

Source: Appendix I

Table 2.4 Bond Deliveries, June 1981

DATE (YYMMDD)	COUPON	MATURITY	NUMBER DELIVERED	FACTOR
810630	13.875	5/15/11-06	2488	1.6287
810630	8.750	11/15/08-03	911	1.0772
810630	9.125	5/15/09-04	480	1.1168
810630	8.375	8/15/08-03	32	1.0385
810630	10.000	5/15 10-05	20	1.2110
810630	12.750	11/15/10-05	9	1.5048
810626	13.875	5/15/11-06	325	1.6287
810625	8.750	11/15/08-03	33	1.0772
810622	13.875	5/15/11-06	1	1.6287
810619	13.875	5/15/11-06	482	1.6287
810619	9.125	5/15/09-04	5	1.1168
810619	7.625	2/15/07-02	2	0.9625
810618	8.750	11/15/08-03	2	1.0772
810618	7.625	2/15/07-02	1	0.9625
810618	10.000	5/15/10-05	1	1.2110
810617	8.750	11/15/08-03	16	1.0772
810617	7.625	2/15/07-02	1	0.9625
810612	8.750	11/15/08-03	60	1.0772
810612	7.625	2/15/07-02	7	0.9625
810611	8.750	11/15/08-03	5	1.0772
810611	10.000	5/15/10-05	1	1.2110
810610	8.750	11/15/08-03	216	1.0772
810610	9.125	5/15/09-04	10	1.1168
810610	8.375	8/15/08-03	3	1.0385
810609	8.750	11/15/08-03	12	1.0772
810609	9.125	5/15/09-04	4	1.1168
810609	8.375	8/15/08-03	2	1.0385
810609	7.625	2/15/07-02	1	0.9625
810608	8.750	11/15/08-03	45	1.0772
810608	7.625	2/15/07-02	6	0.9625
810608	9.125	5/15/09-04	1	1.1168
810608	8.375	8/15/08-03	1	1.0385
810605	8.750	11/15/08-03	188	1.0772
810605	7.625	2/15/07-02	163	0.9625
810605	8.375	8/15/08-03	20	1.0385
810605	9.125	5/15/09-04	14	1.1168
810604	8.750	11/15/08-03	245	1.0772
810604	7.625	2/15/07-02	105	0.9625
810604	8.375	8/15/08-03	26	1.0385
810604	9.125	5/15/09-04	11	1.1168
810603	8.750	11/15/08-03	686	1.0772
810603	7.625	2/15/07-02	254	0.9625
810603	9.125	5/15/09-04	55	1.1168
810603	8.375	8/15/08-03	30	1.0385
810602	8.750	11/15/08-03	1024	1.0772
810602	7.625	2/15/07-02	400	0.9625
810602	8.375	8/15/08-03	46	1.0385
810602	9.125	5/15/09-04	22	1.1168
810601	12.750	11/15/10-05	11	1.5048
Total Deliveries, Average Conversion Factor =			8483	1.2822

Source: Appendix I

Chapter 3

How the Short's Strategic Options Affect the Basis

The person who is short a bond futures contract has two kinds of options—what to deliver and when to deliver it. In practice, these two options take on a variety of forms that owe their richness in part to the complexity of the rules that govern trading and deliveries in the Chicago Board of Trade's futures contract and in part to the complexity of the Treasury securities market itself. This chapter describes the diversity of the short's strategic options.

The Short's Strategic Options

The strategic options available to the person who is short futures include the following:

1. *Actual deliverable bond option.* Deciding which of the existing deliverable bonds to use for actual delivery

2. *Anticipated new issue option.* Using a bond that is expected to be issued by the time of delivery

3. *Wild card option.* Exploiting a price change in the cash market after the futures market has closed

4. *Limit move option.* Exploiting limit moves (in the Chicago Board of Trade's contract) on the first two position days

5. *Major switch option.* Changing deliverable bonds in the last week

of the delivery month after the final settlement price has been determined

6. *Minor switch option.* Changing deliverable bonds between the time of giving notice and the deadline for notification of the actual bond to be delivered

7. *Timing option.* Deciding when in the delivery month to make delivery, which is affected now by the value of the short's options

Value of the Short's Options

These options are valuable to the short and costly to the long. Therefore, the short must pay for the options; the form of that payment is a basis that is higher than carry. For example, on February 19, the 10-3/8s of '12-07 were the cheapest to deliver. At that time, the implied repo rate of those bonds was 3.96 percent, which was substantially less than the 6.65-percent general collateral RP rate then available. The basis of the 10-3/8s of '12-07 was 19/32nds, compared with total carry to the last delivery day of about 8/32nds. Those who were long futures on February 19 required 11/32nds to cover the cost of the short's options.

Source of the Short's Options

The actual deliverable bond option and the anticipated new issues option stem in part from the structure of the Treasury market itself and in part from the rules of the futures contract that allow a wide range of bonds to be delivered. The rest of the options result mainly from how the delivery process and the delivery month are structured. Consider these in turn.

Structure of the Delivery Process

The delivery process requires three business days: Notice Day, Tender Day, and Delivery Day. (See Exhibit 3.1.)

Notice Day   The entire delivery process in Chicago requires three

Exhibit 3.1 Delivery Process in Chicago

	8:00a.m.	Futures Market opens
Notice (Position) Day	2:00p.m.	Futures Market closes
	5:00 (8:00)p.m.	DCNYF deadline for short to give delivery notice (Exchange deadline in parens)
	7:45 (8:30)a.m.	DCNYF deadline for advising long (Exchange deadline in parens)
Tender (Intention) Day	2:00p.m.	Deadline for short to nominate bond to be delivered (Invoice to exchange) Long advised
	3:00p.m.	Deadline for long to give bank information to short
	10:00a.m.	Deadline for short to deliver bond to long's bank
Delivery Day	1:00p.m.	Deadline for long to pay bank for bond

days. The first of these days is called *Notice Day* in the street, although the Board of Trade's official designation is *Position Day*. Whatever it is called, this is the day on which the short gives official notice that delivery will be made. The Exchange's deadline for getting delivery notices from clearing members is 8:00 p.m. Chicago time. Most clearing members set earlier deadlines for getting delivery notices from their customers. Discount Corporation of New York Futures (DCNYF), for example, sets a 5:00 p.m. deadline. The deadline for submitting a notice of delivery falls after the close of the futures market, a timing lag that is the source of the "wild card option."

Tender Day   This second day in the delivery process is called *Tender Day* by DCNYF and *Intention Day* by the Chicago Board of Trade. This is the day the short must say precisely which bond will be used for delivery. The deadline for stating the specific issue is 2:00 p.m., which is almost a full day after the delivery notice is filed. This one-day lag is the source of a one-day "switch option."

Delivery Day   The third day in the delivery process is called *Delivery Day* by everyone. The exchange's deadline for delivering the bond to the long's bank is 10:00 a.m. (Chicago time), and the penalties for missing this deadline are severe. The exchange imposes a $1,000 fine on the short for each futures contract for which the nominated bond is not delivered to the long's bank. Further, the short must make do with whatever bond the exchange chooses to deliver, which need not be the cheapest to deliver. Such a penalty is far more serious than the cost of failing to deliver in the cash Treasury market and is sufficiently large to limit the flexibility of the short in exercising the "switch option."

Delivery Month   Deliveries can be made on any business day during the contract month. (See Exhibit 3.2.) What this means in practice is that the first notice day actually falls on the second business day before

Exhibit 3.2   Delivery Month in Chicago

(Actual Dates for March 1988 Contract)

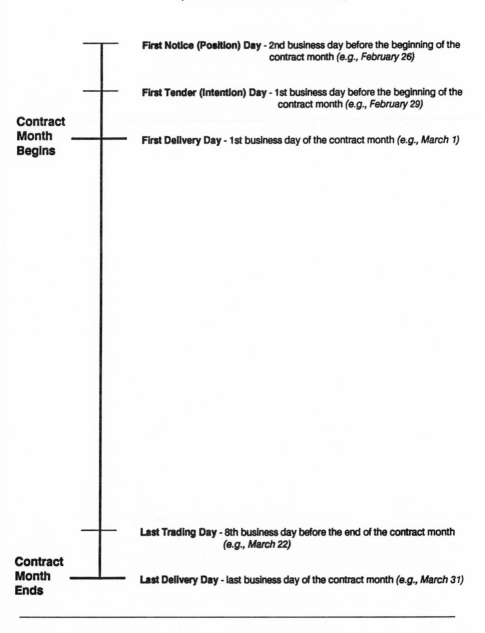

First Notice (Position) Day - 2nd business day before the beginning of the contract month *(e.g., February 26)*

First Tender (Intention) Day - 1st business day before the beginning of the contract month *(e.g., February 29)*

Contract Month Begins

First Delivery Day - 1st business day of the contract month *(e.g., March 1)*

Last Trading Day - 8th business day before the end of the contract month *(e.g., March 22)*

Contract Month Ends

Last Delivery Day - last business day of the contract month *(e.g., March 31)*

the beginning of the contract month. This two-day outcropping provides a variant of the wild card play, stemming in this case from the daily price limits that apply outside the contract month.

Further, because trading stops on the eighth business day before the end of the contract month, deliveries can be made on any day during the seven business days that follow the expiration of trading. The week-long lag between the close of trading and the last possible delivery day is the source of the "switch option."

This comparatively complicated set of arrangements—taken together with the widely varied set of bonds that are eligible for delivery—gives the short plenty of room to maneuver.

Option 1: Actual Deliverable Bond

The cheapest bond to deliver is systematically related to the level of yields. The possibility for changes in the cheapest to deliver combined with the short's right to pick the bond he or she will deliver produce an option that can be quite valuable.

Recall that changes in the cheapest to deliver are caused by changes in the level of yields. Increases in the level of yields tend to make long-duration bonds—that is, those with low coupons and long maturities—cheaper to deliver. Decreases in yields favor short-duration bonds.

To see how the cheapest to deliver option can be valued, consider the following situation. On February 19, yields were trading around 8.5 percent, and the 10-3/8s of '12-07 were the cheapest to deliver. At higher yields, however, the 7-1/4s of '16 would be the cheapest to deliver. At lower yields, the 12-3/4s of '10-05 would be the cheapest to deliver.

Chart 3.1 shows a graph of the converted cash price of each of these three bonds against the various possible levels of yields at the expiration of the March 1988 futures contract. To construct this graph, we

For the purposes of this exercise, we can assume that the futures price divided the cash price of each bond by its own March 1988 conversion factor for yields ranging from 6.66 percent to 10.66 percent.

Chart 3.1 Valuing the Cheapest to Deliver Option

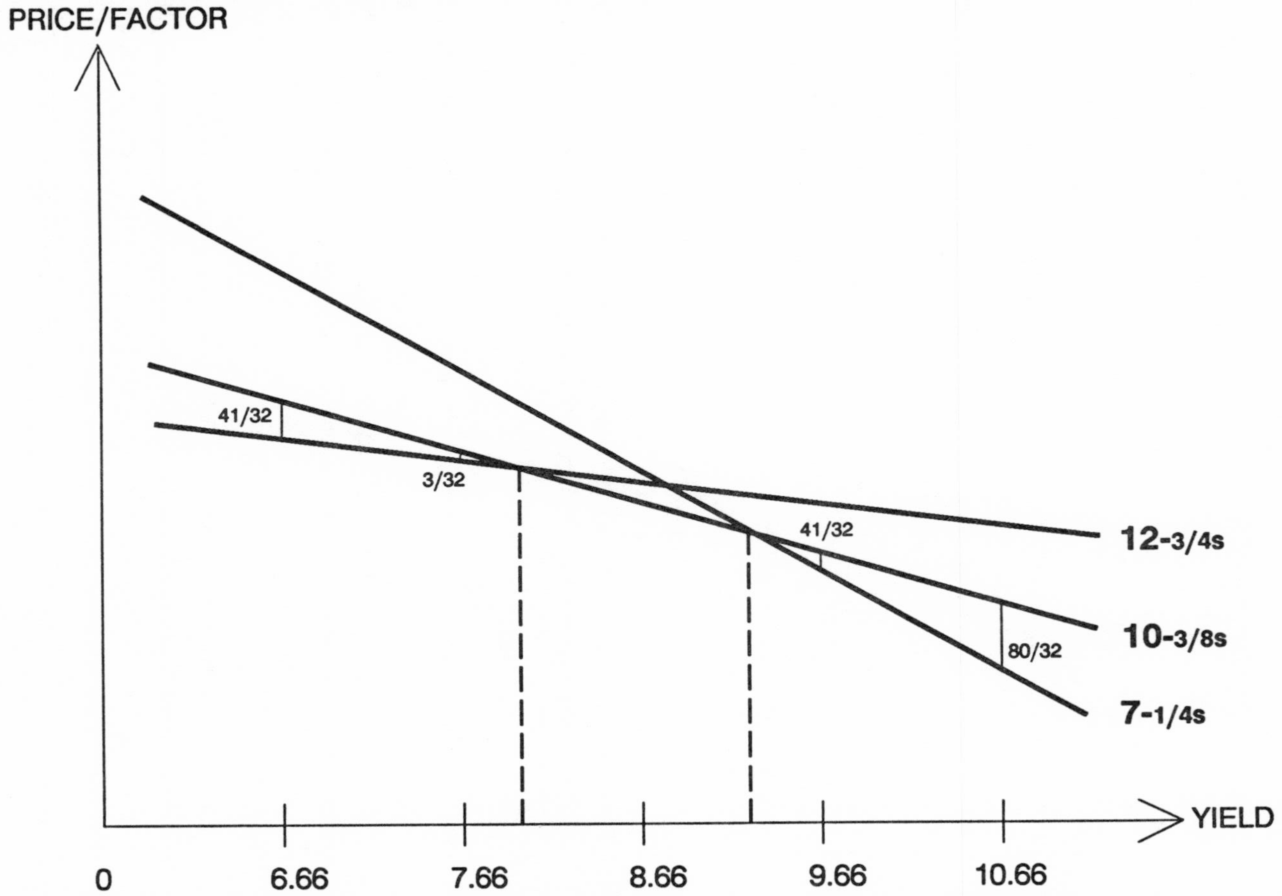

PRICE/FACTOR

12-3/4s

10-3/8s

7-1/4s

80/32

41/32

3/32

41/32

YIELD

0   6.66   7.66   8.66   9.66   10.66

For the purposes of this exercise, we can assume that the futures price is equal to the lowest converted cash price. Thus, for yields in the neighborhood of 8 percent, the converted price of the 10-3/8s of '12-07 will be the futures price. For yields in the neighborhood of 7 percent and below, the converted price of the 12-3/4s of '10-05 will be the futures price. For yields from around 9 percent and higher, the converted price of the 7-1/4s of '16 will be the futures price. (See Table 2.2.)

What this means to whoever is short the futures can be seen by comparing the futures price at each level of yields with what the futures price would have been had the short been locked into delivering the 10-3/8s. For example, if yields go to 9.66 percent at the expiration of futures trading, the futures price based on the 7-1/4s would be 41/32nds lower than the futures price based on the 10-3/8s. At 10.66 percent, the difference is 80/32nds.

On the other hand, if yields fall to 7.66 percent, the short gains 3/32nds from being able to swap out of the 10-3/8s and into the 12-3/4s. At 6.66 percent, the gain would be 41/32nds.

Valuing the option now requires putting probabilities on the various yield outcomes. If yields are comparatively stable, and little time remains until the futures contract expires, the most likely outcome is that the 10-3/8s would remain the cheapest to deliver. If so, the option is worth comparatively little. If yields are volatile, on the other hand, or if there is a great deal of time remaining to the expiration of futures trading, the likelihood of yields rising or falling either 100 or 200 basis points can be quite large. If there is a high probability of a shift in the deliverable bond, the short's option may be quite valuable.

Consider, for example, possible values of the cheapest to deliver option for contracts that have two weeks and three months remaining to expiration. (See Table 3.1.) In the first case, the likelihood of the extreme outcomes of 6.66 percent and 10.66 percent are zero, while the likelihood of the intermediate outcomes of 7.66 percent and 9.66 percent are small. Weighting the value of the option in each case by its respective probability produces an option value of 4/32nds. In the second case, the likelihoods of the extreme outcomes are now positive, and the likelihoods of the intermediate outcomes larger than before. Here, the value of the option would be 19/32nds.

Other Factors in Determining Cheapest to Deliver

There are, of course, other factors than changes in the general level of yields that can cause the cheapest to deliver to change. A temporary squeeze on a particular issue might make it expensive to deliver. A change in the tax code favoring callable bonds might make them expensive to deliver. A change in the slope of the yield curve might make non-callable bonds expensive to deliver. There is no theoretical barrier to bringing these factors into the price of the cheapest to deliver option. The only barrier is hard work.

Table 3.1   Value of the Option to Choose the Cheapest to Deliver

YIELD	OPTION VALUE OF EXPIRATION	PROBABILTIES	
		CASE 1 (2 weeks)	CASE 2 (3 months)
6.66	41/32	0	.05
7.66	3/32	.05	.10
8.66	0/32	.85	.55
9.66	41/32	.10	.20
10.66	80/32	0	.10
OPTION VALUE NOW		4/32nds	19/32nds

Option 2: Anticipated New Issues

The rules of the bond contract allow any U.S. Treasury bond with at least 15 years remaining to first call to be delivered. There is no restriction on when the bond was first issued, and there is no reason why a bond issued between the time the short establishes a position and the time delivery must be made cannot be delivered.

The characteristics of the newly-issued bond cannot be known with certainty, but they can be predicted with increasing accuracy and confidence as the event approaches. First, the date and maturity of the issue are fairly easy to pin down. The U.S. Treasury follows a regular funding cycle with auctions falling on regular dates. It is no accident that the expiration of every deliverable bond falls on the fifteenth of February, May, August, or November.

Second, the Treasury only rarely changes the maturity and call features of the bonds that it issues. For example, the Treasury stopped issuing 30-year issues that were callable with five years remaining to maturity in 1985. At about the same time, they stopped issuing non-callable 20-year bonds. Since then, all of the long-term bonds have been 30-year bonds with no call privileges.

Thus, traders can predict the maturity of a new issue with considerable precision. What is more difficult is predicting the coupon of the issue. The Treasury tends to set the coupon for a new issue so that the issue's initial price will be at or slightly below par. What can only be guessed is the level of yields at the time the auction.

Even so, valuing the anticipated new issue option is no more difficult than valuing the cheapest to deliver option. All that needs to be done is to select a range of yields, which can be used as the coupon of the new issue, to assign probabilities to each yield outcome, and to value the gain to the short of being able to switch into the newly issued bond.

Going through all of these motions, however, shows only that the short's anticipated new issue option is worth comparatively little. At high yields, for example, the new issue will have a high coupon. But high yields favor the delivery of long-duration bonds, and the high coupon will tend to give the newly-issued bond a low duration: the new bond would probably not be the cheapest to deliver if yields are high. Similarly, if yields are low, the new bond would have a low coupon. But low yields favor the delivery of short-duration bonds, and the low coupon on the new issue would tend to give it a long duration.

Further, new issues tend to trade at slightly lower yields simply because they are "on the run" and liquid.

As a result, the anticipated new issue option usually is worth comparatively little. The chief exception to this rule occurred several years ago in the note futures contract when yields were high but falling. The high yields meant that long-duration notes were favored for delivery while the falling yields meant that the "new guy" had both the lowest coupon and longest maturity combining to produce the longest duration of any note in the deliverable set. Thus, for a time, the anticipated new issue played an important role in setting note futures prices. Since then, this option has played no role in either the bond or note futures contracts.

Occasionally, the Treasury chooses to reopen an existing issue—that is, add to the supply of an existing bond—rather than auction a new bond with its own coupon and maturity. As things now stand (May 1988), such reopenings seem to have no net effect on the basis of the issue that is reopened. On the one hand, the increased supply should depress the price somewhat. But the additional supply also tends to keep the bond "on the run," which means that it continues to be actively traded by government securities dealers. The net effect appears to be a wash in terms of basis and yield.

Option 3: Wild Card Play

With rare exceptions, the combined effect of net carry and the value of the short's various options is a positive basis for the cheapest to deliver. Making delivery before the last delivery day of the contract month means giving up the basis on the bond that is delivered. As long as the basis is positive, then, most shorts will plan to wait until the last delivery day to make their deliveries.

Occasionally, however, circumstances conspire to make it worth the short's while to give up the basis and to make delivery early. In a positive carry setting, a *wild card delivery* is an early delivery prompted by price movements in the cash market after the futures market closes for the day. (In a negative carry setting, anticipation of the wild card can postpone delivery.) The opportunity does not arise often, but when it does, it can be quite profitable.

Key Ingredients for the Wild Card

Opportunities to play the wild card are produced by the interaction of the following:

- The deadline for giving notice of delivery is several hours after the futures settlement price of the day is determined
- The conversion factors for most deliverable bonds differ from 1.000
- Futures are marked to market

Wild Card Example

Consider the following set of circumstances for a trader who is long the basis at the close of trading on any day except the last day of trading in the futures.

- The trader is long $1 million par value of the cheapest to deliver, which is a bond that has a conversion factor for the lead futures month of 1.500
- The trader is short 15 futures
- The decimal price of the bond at 2:00 Chicago time is 147.5938
- The decimal futures price at the close of trading is 98.0938

- Given an invoice price of 147.1407, the basis of the cheapest to deliver is .4531, or $4531 per million par value of the cheapest to deliver

Now suppose that after the futures market closes, a bearish piece of news hits the wire and the price of the cheapest to deliver falls two full points in late afternoon trading.

As long as the drop in the market takes place before the deadline for filing notice of intent to deliver, the short has two possible courses of action:

- Wait until the next trading day when the futures price will be lower because of the drop in cash prices.
- Buy $0.5 million par value of the cheapest to deliver and make delivery on all 15 short futures contracts.

In this example, each futures contract calls for the delivery of $100,000 par value of the bonds delivered. To make delivery on 15 short futures, the short needs the addition $0.5 million par value of the bonds to make up the difference between what he or she has and what he or she needs.

Choosing the Delivery Date   Which course of action the short chooses depends on which yields the higher net gain. Compare the results of the two approaches, keeping in mind that whatever the short does, the value of the long bonds has fallen by $20,000.

If the short waits until the next trading day, the short futures will probably show a slight gain. If there is no change in the basis, the two-point drop in the price of the cheapest to deliver should translate into a 1-11/32 [= 2/1.5000] drop in the futures price. The short can expect the futures price to track the decline in the price of the cheapest to deliver.

The value of the drop to someone who is short 15 futures is about $20,000. To capture this $20,000, the short can either trade out of the position when futures open the next day, or stay in the position and collect a mark-to-market payment after the close of business the next day.

By waiting, the short's expected gain on futures is $20,000.

If the short decides instead to make delivery, he or she will buy $0.5 million of the cheapest to deliver and then sell $1.5 million par value of the bonds at an invoice price of 147.1406 [= 1.5000 × 98.0938]. Because the bonds have a market value of 145.5938, the gain to making delivery is

$23,200 [= 15 × (147.1406 − 145.5938)].

By making the delivery immediately, the short's gain is $23,200.

Therefore, the net gain by playing the wild card is $3,200.

In this instance, the short should be willing to give up the expected basis on the bond and the expected mark-to-market payment to take advantage of being able to sell the bonds at a price well above the current cash market.

What if the bond's price had fallen only 1 point?

A price change after the close of futures is not by itself enough to prompt a wild card delivery. If the price of the cheapest to deliver had fallen only one point instead of two, the comparison would have been quite different. The expected decrease in the futures price (assuming again no change in the basis) would be only half as large as in the first example. **The expected gain from waiting would be $10,000.**

The difference between the futures invoice price and the market price of the cheapest to deliver would be a full point less than in the first example. Note, though, that the effect on the difference is disproportionately large. The price of the bond has fallen by half as much as in the first example, but the difference between the invoice and market prices will have fallen by more than half as much. If the short delivers $1.5 million of the cheapest to deliver, the gain would be $8,200 = [15 × (147.1406 − 146.5938)].

The gain from making immediate delivery would be $8,200.

Therefore, the net gain from playing the wild card is –$1,800.

In this case, the drop in cash bond prices is not large enough to trigger a wild card play.

What drives the wild card play?

To make delivery rather than wait, the short needs enough bonds to deliver $100,000 par value of the bonds on each futures contract. In the example above, the trader is long $1 million par value of the cheapest to deliver and short C, or 1.5000, futures for each $100,000. Making up the difference then requires buying (C − 1), or 0.5000, bonds for each bond in the original position.

The difference between C and 1 is known as the "tail."

In the example, the tail is 0.5000. Had the tail been much smaller, a two-point drop in price might not have been enough to make delivery the more profitable choice. Suppose, instead, that the conversion factor of the cheapest to deliver bond had been 1.000 (and so had no tail at all). Suppose further that the decimal price of the bond at the close of futures trading is 98.5625 and the basis is still 15/32nds, so the settlement futures price is 98.0938.

A two-point drop in the price of the cheapest to deliver will now produce an expected two-point drop in the futures. But the trader is short only 10 futures for each $1 million long bonds in the position. As a result, the expected gain from waiting would still be $20,000.

The gain from electing to make delivery, however, would yield only $15,313, which is the difference between the invoice price of the bonds (98.0938) and the new market price of the bonds (96.5625) for $1 million par value of the bonds. Without a large positive tail to take advantage of, the short's best choice is to wait.

In general, the rule for determining whether a drop in cash prices after the close of futures trading prompts a wild card play is:

Cash price decrease > [C/(C − 1)] × Basis

for bonds with conversion factors greater than 1.000.[*]

In the initial example, the conversion factor was 1.5000 and the basis of the bond was 15/32nds. To prompt a wild card delivery, then, the decrease in the cash price of the bond would have to be at least 45/32nds = [1.5000/(1.5000 − 1)] × 15/32nds. A two-point drop was enough, while a one-point drop was too small.

The rule also shows that for bonds with a conversion factor of 1.000, no price decrease is large enough to make a wild card play worthwhile.

In principle, there is no reason a price increase cannot produce a wild card. In this case, an increase in cash prices after the close of futures trading prompts a wild card if

Cash price increase > [C/(1 − C)] × Basis

for bonds with conversion factors less than 1.000. As a practical matter, though, the factors of the bonds that are now currently eligible for delivery are too close to 1.000 for a wild card play to be prompted by price increases. For this reason, we leave it to the interested *and* compulsive reader to prove that a price increase can lead to a wild card play.

Intuition Behind the Wild Card

The intuition behind the wild card is that a dollar in the futures price at settlement is worth C dollars to the short at delivery. When a price move occurs after the settlement price is determined but before the delivery notice deadline, the short can do one of two things: (1) get one dollar per dollar in the futures price change by waiting and marking to market or (2) get C dollars per dollar by deciding to deliver immediately. The gain from making the wild card delivery needs to exceed the basis that the short must give up by effecting immediate delivery.

---

[*]   For the derivation of this rule, see "T-Bond Deliveries and the 'Wild Card' " by David Emanuel, John Finn, and Morton Lane, DCNYF Occasional Research Paper No. 786.

Switching the Delivered Bond on a Wild Card

The wild card strategy favors the delivery of bonds with high conversion factors and low bases. The cheapest to deliver has the lowest basis in most cases, and if it has a high conversion factor as well, then the cheapest to deliver is the most likely candidate for a wild card delivery.

The price move can be large enough, though, to make it worthwhile to swap out of the cheapest to deliver and into a bond with a higher conversion factor even if the basis for that bond is higher. To check this possibility, one should compute the gain from the wild card delivery for several other deliverable bonds with higher conversion factors. The short should then deliver the bond that provides the highest gain from the wild card delivery, providing of course that the non-cheap bond can be procured in time to effect delivery by 10:00 a.m. Chicago time on delivery day. (See the Switch Option for more on the importance of being able to lay your hands on the bonds you intend to deliver.)

A Real-Life Wild Card Example

Wild card plays have been infrequent in the U.S. over the past several years, mostly because the time between the close of the futures market and the time delivery notice must be tendered is comparatively short for the Chicago Board of Trade and because the cash bond market in the U.S. is fairly quiet after the futures market closes.

To find a good example of a wild card play, therefore, we must turn to LIFFE (London International Financial Futures Exchange), which also trades a Treasury bond futures contract, and look back to 1986. At that time, there were two important differences between LIFFE's and the CBOT's contracts:

- The amount of time between the close of LIFFE's market and the deadline for submitting a delivery notice was considerably longer than at the Chicago Board of Trade.
- The time during which the short could play the wild card at LIFFE was mid-morning in the United States, which typically is an active trading time for Treasury bonds. (LIFFE has since changed

its rules so that the settlement price and delivery procedures are identical to those of the Chicago Board of Trade, including an adherence to Chicago's timetable.)

On May 29, 1986 the LIFFE Exchange Delivery Settlement Price (EDSP) was determined at 4:00 p.m. London time (9:00 a.m. Chicago time) to be 96-18/32. The 14s of 11/11-06 were the cheapest to deliver and were trading at that time for about 154-20/32 and had a conversion factor of 1.5965. Thus, the basis of the 14s was

Basis = $154.625 - 1.5965 \times 96.5625 = 0.4630$

or about 15/32nds.

Later that day, the futures in Chicago were down limit, while the cash market continued to fall. At around 2:30 p.m. Chicago time, the deadline at the time for giving notice of delivery on LIFFE, the 14s were trading in the cash market for about 152-1/32.

Consider the choices facing someone who was short 160 LIFFE futures against a long position of $10 million par value of the 14s. If the short decides to wait, the gain on his or her short futures position is likely to equal the decrease in the market value of the bonds. That is, the expected gain for waiting would have been about $260 thousand.

If the short decides to deliver, he or she would first have to buy $6 million of the 14s at a price of 152-1/32 (ignoring accrued interest). Delivering the entire $16 million at the futures invoice price then provides a net of 160 x $[(1.5965 \times 96.5625) - 152.03125]$ = $340,925. That is, the known gain to making immediate delivery was about $340 thousand. In other words, the short picked up an extra $80 thousand by playing the wild card.

Option 4: Limit Move

The expiring bond contract at the Chicago Board of Trade has no price limits in its delivery month. However, the first two notice days occur in the preceding month and are governed by price limits.

The principal effect of a limit move is to accelerate the closing time for the market to the time at which the market last hits and stays at the limit. When this happens, the wild card play has more time to develop. Because these conditions are only in place for two days, this variant of the wild card option adds comparatively little to the anticipated value of wild card opportunities.

Option 5: Major Switch

Once the futures have closed on the last day of trading, the settlement price used in calculating delivery invoices is fixed. Even so, substantial changes in cash prices may occur during the seven days between the last day of trading and the last delivery day. As a result, the cheapest bond to deliver may change between the time futures trading stops and the last possible delivery day. In a sufficiently volatile market, the deliverable bond can change more than once during this period.

The forces that drive the switch option are quite a bit different from the forces that drive the shift in the deliverable bond that can take place while futures are still trading. One peculiar result of these differences is that a change in yields that would make a bond cheap to deliver while futures are still trading will tend to make the bond expensive to deliver once futures trading has expired. (The resolution to this paradox is provided at the end of this section.)

Fixing the settlement price at the expiration of futures trading has one immediate implication. That is, hedge ratios must be adjusted. Each short futures position that remains open after the close of trading calls for the delivery of $100,000 par value of eligible bonds irrespective of the bonds' market price. The correct ratio is then one-to-one after the close of trading rather than C futures contracts for each $100,000 par value of bonds, where C is the conversion factor. The invoice price is fixed once trading stops for good.

During the week between the last day of trading and the last delivery day, the short can exploit the use of conversion factors with a vengeance. The resulting switch option can be quite valuable, even though it lasts only a week.

How the Switch Option Works

To see how the switch option works, suppose that the information in Table 3.2 describes the situation on the last trading day of the contract month (for example, March 22, 1988). The information presented there includes the following:

- **Bond** includes the coupon and maturity of the three bonds considered, the 10-3/8s of '12, the 12s of '13, and the 7-1/4s of '16
- **Basis less Carry on Last Trading Day** is reckoned using total carry to the last delivery day
- **Ticks per Basis Point Change in Yield** is a measure of the absolute price sensitivity of each bond expressed in 32nds
- **Price Change** shows the total change in price of each bond for a 25-basis-point decrease and a 25-basis-point increase in yields

Note that the 10-3/8s are the cheapest to deliver of the three bonds shown because the cost to the short is 4/32nds, which is four ticks in the futures. The difference between the basis of the 10-3/8s on the last trading day and the carry remaining to the last delivery day is 4/32nds or four ticks. The basis of the 12s is shown to be six ticks over carry, and the basis of the 7-1/4s is eight ticks over carry.

Change in the Cheapest to Deliver   Although the 10-3/8s are the cheapest to deliver on the last trading day, a large enough change in yields can cause either the 12s or the 7-1/4s to be the cheapest to deliver. Consider the distance between the 10-3/8s and the 12s. The difference in the net bases of the two bonds is 2/32nds. If the price of the 12s were to fall 2/32nds relative to the price of the 10-3/8s, the two bonds would be equally cheap to deliver. If the price of the 12s were to fall more than 2/32nds relative to the price of the 10-3/8s, it would pay to switch out of the 10-3/8s and into the 12s.

Table 3.2 Assessing the Switch Option

BOND	BASIS LESS CARRY ON LAST TRADING DAY*	TICK PER BASIS POINT CHANGE IN YIELD**	PRICE CHANGE	
			YIELDS FALL (-25 bps)	YIELDS RISE (+25 bps)
10-3/8s of 12	4	-3.33/32nds	+83/32	-83/32
12s of 13	6	-3.79/32nds	+95/32	-95/32
7-1/4s of 16	8	-2.97/32nds	+74/32	-74/32

* Carry is total to last delivery day

** Dollar value of a basis point expressed in 32nds. The inverse of the yield value of a 32nd.

If we assume that yield spreads between bonds do not change, we can determine how much yields would have to change and in what direction, using the information on price sensitivity shown in the third column of Table 3.2. Each basis-point increase in yields causes the price of the 10-3/8s to fall by 3.33/32nds. Each basis-point increase in yields causes the price of the 12s to fall by 3.79/32nds. In other words, the price of the 12s will fall 0.46/32nds per basis point faster than the price of the 10-3/8s if yields rise. In other words, a 1-basis-point increase in yields causes the price of the 12s to fall 0.46/32nds relative to the price of the 10-3/8s.

The initial basis of the 12s is 2/32nds larger than the basis of the 10-3/8s. For the 12s to be as cheap to deliver as the 10-3/8s, then, the price of the 12s must fall 2/32nds relative to the price of the 10-3/8s. To cover this distance, yields must rise by 4.35 basis points [= 2/.46]. If yields rise by more than 4.35 basis points, the 12s become the cheaper to deliver, and a switch should be made.

By the same reasoning, we find that a decrease in yields can cause the 7-1/4s to become the cheapest to deliver. In this case, if the price of the 10-3/8s increases four ticks relative to the price of the 7-1/4s, the two will be equally cheap to deliver. Comparing the price responsiveness of the two bonds, we find that each basis point decrease in yields causes the price of the 10-3/8s to rise 0.36/32nds [= (3.33 − 2.97)/32nds] relative to the price of the 7-1/4s. To cover a distance of 4/32nds would then require yields to fall by 11.11 basis points [= 4/.36]. Any further decrease in yields would cause the 7-1/4s to become the cheapest to deliver, and a switch should be made.

Cost and Return   To establish a long position in the switch option, the trader sells one futures contract for each $100,000 par value of the 10-3/8s. The total cost of the option is simply the difference between the basis of the 10-3/8s on the last trading day and total carry to the last trading day. In the example, the cost is 4/32nds, or four ticks per futures contract.

If yields do not change, the 10-3/8s will stay the cheapest to deliver, and the option expires worthless for a net loss of four ticks for each short futures.

If yields rise 4.35 basis points, the 10-3/8s and the 12s are equally cheap, but the option still expires worthless. If yields fall 11.11 basis points, the 10-3/8s and the 7-1/4s are equally cheap, but the option expires worthless.

If yields rise more than 4.35 basis points, it pays to switch out of the 10-3/8s and into the 12s. For example, if yields rise 25 basis points (see the table), the price of the 12s will fall 12/32nds more than the price of the 10-3/8s. The trader only needed two to make the switch and another four to cover the cost of the switch option. Thus, the trader profits 6/32nds.

If yields fall more than 11.11 basis points, it pays to switch out of the 10-3/8s and into the 7-1/4s. For example, a 25-basis-point fall in yields causes the price of the 10-3/8s to rise by 9/32nds more than the price of the 7-1/4s. The trader needed 4/32nds to make the switch and another 4/32nds to cover the cost of the option. In this case, the net profit is 1/32nd for each option

What Drives the Switch Option? What causes a change in the cheapest to deliver after the expiration of a futures contract is the *absolute* change in the prices of competing bonds. In the current example, when yields fell and prices rose, the bond whose price rose the least became the cheapest to deliver. When yields rose and prices fell, it was the bond whose price fell the most that became the cheapest to deliver.

This is quite different from the shift in the deliverable bond that can take place when yields change while futures are still trading. When futures are still trading, it is the *relative* change in the price of the bond that matters.

The difference leads to some interesting comparisons. For example, when futures are still trading, a decrease in yields tends to make low-duration bonds cheaper to deliver. In this case, though, it was the 7-

1/4s, which have a comparatively high duration, that became cheaper because the absolute change in the price of the 7-1/4s was smaller than the absolute change in the price of the 10-3/8s. (The relative change in the price of the 7-1/4s, though, was still greater than the relative change in the price of the 10-3/8s.)

Similarly, when futures are still trading, an increase in yields tends to make high-duration bonds cheaper to deliver. In this case, however, it was the 12s that became cheap because the price of the 12s is absolutely more responsive to yield changes than is the price of either the 10-3/8s or the 7-1/4s.

For those who like rules of thumb, Charts 3.2 and 3.3 provide an interesting comparison. Chart 3.2 plots the durations of bonds that are eligible for delivery against their respective coupons. As one would expect, high coupons generally mean low durations. Chart 3.3 plots the dollar value of a basis point against coupon for the eligible bonds. Here we find that high coupons generally mean high price responsiveness.

As a rule, the forces that drive the switch option are nearly the mirror image of the forces that drive the normal shift in the deliverable bond. If a yield increase tends to make the 7-1/4s cheap to deliver when futures are still trading, the same yield increase would tend to make the 7-1/4s relatively expensive to deliver after the futures contract has expired. In contrast, a yield decrease after futures trading has expired would tend to make the 7-1/4s, which have a low coupon and a comparatively low absolute price-responsiveness to yield changes, cheaper to deliver.

Value of Major Switch Option The value of the switch option depends on the possibility of changes in the cheapest to deliver during the week or so left in the contract month after trading in the expiring futures contract has stopped. It is most likely to come into play when two or more bonds approach expiration with similar bases and those bonds have prices that, when divided through by their respective conversion factors, exhibit substantially different absolute responsiveness to changes in the level of yields.

Chart 3.2 Bond Coupon vs. Duration (April 26, 1988)

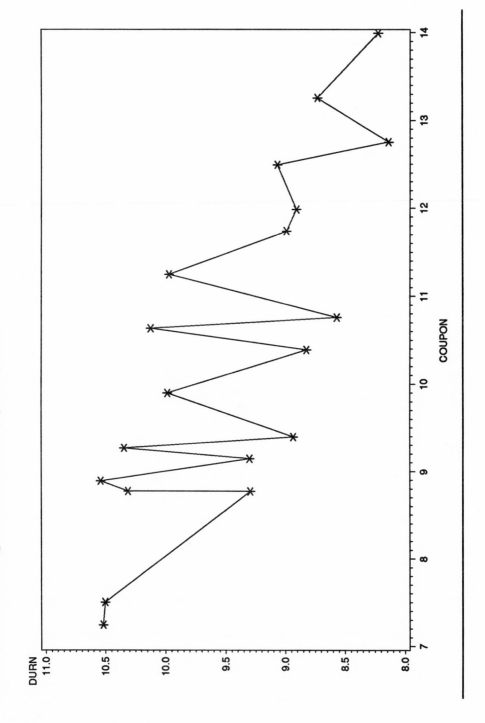

Chart 3.3 Bond Coupon vs. $/BP (April 26, 1988)

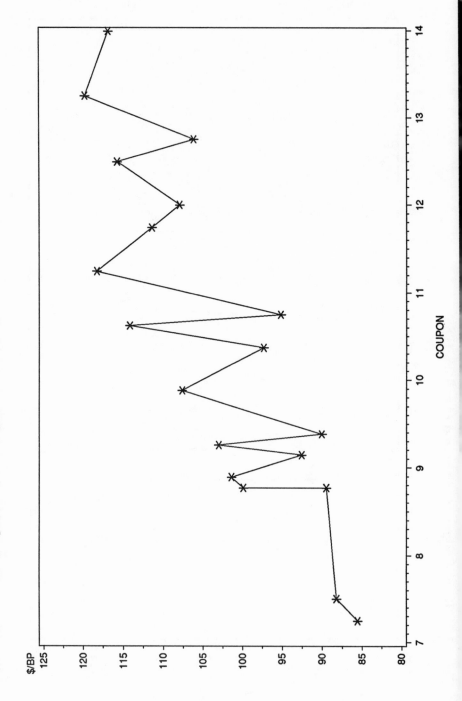

Major Switch Option Example

The following example puts the cost of a switch option and its payoff into dollars.

June 1986 futures settled at 96-13/32nds (or 96.40625) on June 19, which was the last day of futures trading in the expiring contract. (See Table 3.3.) The 12-1/2s of '14 were the cheapest to deliver, and the 12s of '13 were a close second. One could buy the 12-1/2 basis for approximately 7/32nds, which is about the same as its basis at the close on June 18.

The negative basis figures shown for the 12s and the 12-1/2s on June 19 reflect differences in the time of day at which the futures and bond prices were taken on that day. On the last day of trading, the expiring futures contract closes at 12:00 noon in Chicago, while trading in all other futures contracts continues until the normal closing at 2:00 p.m. Chicago time. On June 19, 1986, between noon and 2:00 p.m., which is when we collect our data on bond prices, prices in the bond market fell substantially.

Cost of the Major Switch Option   To buy the switch option, you must first buy the basis of the cheapest to deliver bond at expiration, selling 10 futures for each $1 million par value of the bonds purchased. An alternative, of course, is simply to keep a long basis position with the cheapest to deliver at expiration, adjusting the hedge ratio to 10 short futures for each $1 million par value of bonds in the position just before trading in the futures contract expires.

The cost of the option is the difference between the basis at futures expiration and any net carry between the last trading day and the last delivery day. In this case, the initial basis of the 12-1/2s is $2,400 per $1 million. At a financing cost of 6.5 percent, the 12-1/2s has a positive carry of $522 per $1 million.

As a practical matter, it is often prudent to keep the bonds that will be delivered at the bank during the past couple of days before delivery is made. Doing so may result in a slightly lower value for positive carry, but only slightly, while it eliminates the possibility of failing to deliver.

Table 3.3 Switch Option Illustration—June 1986 Delivery Cycle (6/19/86 Futures Settlement = 96.40625)

INVOICE PRICE DATA

Coupon	10-3/8	12	12-1/2
Maturity	11/15/12	5/15/13	8/15/14
Factor	1.2406	1.4110	1.4699
Invoice Price*	119.602	136.029	141.708

* At 6/19/86 Futures Settlement, excluding accrued interest.

CASH PRICE AND BASIS DATA*

DATE	CASH PRICE			BASIS		
	10-3/8	12-00	12-1/2	10-3/8	12-00	12-1/2
6/18/86	121.625	137.563	143.281	0.90	0.25	0.24
6/19/86	120.125	135.594	141.188	0.52	-0.44	-0.52
6/20/86	122.000	138.219	143.719	2.40	2.19	2.01
6/23/86	122.938	139.156	144.938	3.34	3.13	3.23
6/24/86	123.344	139.531	145.375	3.74	3.50	3.67
6/25/86	123.250	139.563	145.531	3.65	3.53	3.82
6/26/86	123.406	139.750	145.563	3.80	3.72	3.86
6/27/86	124.031	140.750	146.719	4.43	4.72	5.01

* Cash bond prices are taken at 2.00pm (CST)
  All values are in decimal
** Negative basis reflects comparison of 12:00pm futures price with 2:00pm cash bond price.

Recall that the CBOT's penalties for failing to deliver are extreme and possibly draconian.

The net cost of the switch option per $1 million par value of the bonds was then

Basis on last trading day	$2,400
Net carry to last delivery day	(522)
Cost of the switch option	$1,878

Payoff to the Major Switch Option Trading in the expiring futures contract stops at noon on the last trading day. (Trading in all other contracts continues as usual until 2:00.) By 2:00 Friday on the afternoon of the 19th, cash bond prices had fallen so that the June basis of the 12-1/2s was –0.52, or –$5,200 per million. Note that the 12-1/2s were still the cheapest to deliver, although the 10-3/8s appear to have been temporarily just as cheap.

Bonds began to rally on the 20th and continued to rise more or less without interruption through the 27th. The price of the 12-1/2s rose more than the prices of the other two bonds so that, by the 25th, the switch option was fairly well in the money. The holder of the switch option could switch out of the 12-1/2s and into the 12s for a gross gain of 0.29 = [3.82 − 3.53] per million or $2,900. Given the initial $1,878 cost of the option, the net payoff to the switch option was $1,022.

Practical Consideration

Throughout the week-long rally, the 10-3/8s were becoming cheaper and by the 27th had become cheaper than the 12s. By the 27th, however, it is too late to make the switch. The rules of the Chicago Board of Trade require that bonds be delivered by 10:00 the morning of delivery. Under regular settlement in a bond transaction, the bond is not received via Fed wire until 2:00 the afternoon following the trade. Therefore, if one were to sell the 12s that were bought as part of the first swap and purchase the 10-3/8s on Friday the 27th, the 10-3/8s would not be available in time to make delivery on the contract.

Even if what should be ample time is allowed to receive the bonds, the seller of the bonds can still fail to deliver.

To protect against a failure to deliver (a *fail*), the switch option trader can hold the original bonds until receiving the new bonds. If the new bonds don't arrive on time, the worst that can happen is that the trader delivers the original bonds and the valuable switch option remains unexercised. Thus, the cost of a fail is a foregone opportunity to exercise a valuable switch option.

The delivery schedule raises a related question regarding bond deliveries that underscores the need to understand the cash bond market thoroughly before undertaking a trade of this kind. The seller of a bond can fail to deliver, and fails are likely if a bond is in short supply. There are penalties for failing to deliver, but these penalties pale in comparison with the penalties imposed by the Chicago Board of Trade for failing to make delivery into a futures contract. Thus, one should know that the bonds are readily available before making a switch.

Multiple Exercise of Major Switch Option

If the price change on the 27th had occurred on the 26th instead, and if the trader were confident that the 10-3/8s were available, a second switch could made. In this case, switching out of the 12s and into the 10-3/8s would add an additional 0.29 [= 4.72 − 4.43] or $2,900 per million to the payoff on the switch option.

If prices had fallen substantially on the 26th, the trader might well have switched back into the 12-1/2s. There is no theoretical limit to the number of times that the switch option can be exercised. This is good news to the holder of the switch option and bad news (unless you are a graduate students seeking an exotic research problem) for whoever is given the task of determining the theoretically correct price of the switch option.

Option 6: Minor Switch

Notice of delivery must be given two business days before the bonds are actually delivered, but the short has almost a whole day after he or she gives notice of delivery to decide which actual bond to deliver. Since the settlement price is already determined, the short has a very short-term option of the type he or she has after the last trading day. Because it lasts less than a day, it has only a very small value.

Option 7: Timing

In addition to deciding *which* bond to deliver, the short decides *when* to make delivery. Delivery can take place on any business day in the delivery month.

Generally, the decision to deliver at the start or end of the delivery month is dictated by the repo (financing) rate on the bond that is cheapest to deliver. If the repo rate is less than the current yield on the bond, there will be positive carry. A position that is long cash and short futures will have positive cash flow, and the inclination will be to defer delivery. Conversely, when there is negative carry, it will probably pay to deliver at the start of the delivery month. However, by delivering early, the short gives up the remaining value of her or his other delivery options. So, the short might defer delivery even if there is slightly negative carry.

If the repo rate is higher than the coupon yield, delivering at the beginning of the month rather than at the end saves a month's worth of negative carry. For example, if the repo rate is 100 basis points higher than the coupon yield, a month's negative carry amounts to about eight basis points [= 100/12 months], or 0.08 percent of the futures invoice price.

How much the timing option is worth then depends on how negatively-sloped the yield curve is at the beginning of the contract month and on the likelihood of each possible negative slope. For example, during the period from late 1979 through 1982, the slope of the yield curve was highly volatile, and the likelihood of large negative slopes was far from trivial. Over the past several years, the yield curve has kept its positive slope, and the timing option has been worthless at every expiration as a result.

The first step in valuing the timing option is to determine the value of the option at the first notice day, which is when the option—if it has value—would be most valuable. Recall that the timing option gets its value from avoiding negative carry. The sooner the option is exercised, the more negative carry is avoided. If we start with a positively-sloped yield curve, each percentage point worth of negative slope in the yield curve is worth about 0.08 percent of the futures invoice price.

The second step is to assign likelihoods to each yield curve slope. Once this is done, we can calculate the value of the option as a simple weighted average of the various expiration values of the option. For the example shown in Table 3.4, the value of the option at this stage would be 0.02 percent of the futures invoice price. If the cheapest to deliver were at par, the value of the option would be about 1/32nd.

Complicating Factors for Various Options

There remains one problem in valuing the various timing and switch options that we have not discussed. The various options are all at the same time related to one another and mutually exclusive.

- Yield curve outcomes that favor one option may take away from the value of another.
- Exercising any one of the options means giving up the value of all the other options.

For example, if the timing option is exercised and delivery is made early, the short must give up the wild card and switch options. If the wild card option is exercised, the switch option must be foregone, and so forth.

Table 3.4 Valuing the Timing Option

SLOPE OF THE YIELD CURVE (Basis Points)*	EXERCISE VALUE OF THE OPTION ON FIRST NOTICE DAY	PROBABILITY OF YIELD CURVE SLOPE	PROBABILITY OF EXERCISE
	(% of Futures Invoice Price)		
300	0	.26	0
200	0	.24	0
100	0	.20	0
0	0	.14	0
-100	.08	.09	?
-200	.16	.05	?
-300	.24	.02	?

* Yield on cheapest to deliver less general collateral RP rate.

Dealing with these complications is beyond the scope of this book, but they are clearly worth keeping in mind when deciding on a basis strategy.

Chapter 4

Practical Considerations in Trading the Basis

Everyone who trades the basis comes face to face with a wide range of real-world problems. Some of these we have mentioned in passing already. Five important issues come up regularly:

- RP specials
- Term financing versus overnight financing
- Basis of a non-cheap bond
- Short squeeze
- Delivery month

The *RP specials* and *term financing versus overnight financing* issues involve the cost of financing a long bond position or the return to invested funds that one can earn on the proceeds of a bond sale. The profit margins in a basis trade are not necessarily large, and what may seem to be the mundane problem of daily financing can make the difference between profitable and unprofitable basis trades.

The *basis of a non-cheap bond* issue arises because the basis of a bond other than the cheapest to deliver—a *non-cheap bond*—is actually a bundled trade that depends both on the basis of the cheapest to deliver and on the price spread between the non-cheap bond and the cheapest to deliver. Because conversion factors do not measure absolute price sensitivity very well, basis trades involving non-cheap bonds require special attention—as do hedges for non-cheap bonds.

Small short squeezes occur frequently in issues that have small public supplies or that have been salted away in portfolios for years. Major short squeezes occur rarely, but when they do the results can be staggering. In the section on short squeezes, we will tell about the spring of 1986 and the squeeze of the 9-1/4s of '16.

All of the timing and delivery options become eligible for exercise during the delivery month. Delivery becomes a real possibility, and the basis trader must weigh the alternatives of closing out the trade, rolling the futures leg of the trade into the next contract month, or going through to delivery.

RP Specials

In the example of selling the basis with the 12s of '13, the reverse RP rate was a major factor in the total profits of the trade. That example assumed the reverse RP rate was 6.65 percent. In the real world, things are not so simple. To understand the RP market, it is important to distinguish between General Collateral and Specials.

- *General collateral*, or *Stock*, is whatever Treasury issues are readily available to be lent or borrowed, typically somewhat below that day's Federal Funds rate.
- A *Special* is a request to borrow a specific Treasury issue. Specials can trade at RP rates substantially lower than the rate for general collateral. If the reverse RP for a particular bond is below the general collateral RP rate, the bond is said to be "on special."

When you sell short the cash market versus futures, you kill two birds with one stone by "reversing in" the particular bond you are short. The first is that you get a bond that allows you to make good on your short sale. The second is that you invest the proceeds of your short sale.

In a reverse RP transaction, you buy the issue with an agreement to sell the issue back at a predetermined price at a later date. What you earn on the transaction is called the reverse repo rate.

If the specific issue that you are looking for is not readily available, the reverse repo rate on the specific issue may be several percentage points below the general collateral reverse repo rate. At times, an issue cannot be found at all, and the short must to fail to deliver. In such a case, the short pays the coupon interest on the issue that he or she is short, and earns no reverse repo interest at all.

Formally, whenever you specify a particular issue in a reverse RP transaction, you are requesting a "special." In practice, though, the particular bond is said to be "on special" only if the reverse RP rate is below the general collateral rate.

RP Special Example

A particularly vivid example of the importance of a bond's being "on special" springs from January and February of 1987 (trade dates 1/27/87 – 2/24/87). The average reverse repo rate on the 14s of '11 for the period was about 2.0 percent. Meanwhile, the 12s of '13 traded between 4.75 percent and 5.5 percent, with an average reverse repo rate of about 5.0 percent. The choice of the 12s of '13 instead of the 14s of '11 as a short sale versus futures worked out well as a result. In part the choice stemmed from the fact that $14.755 billion of the 12s was outstanding, compared with only $4.901 billion of the 14s.

The basis of the 12s fell from 55-1/2 to 33-1/2 (or 22/32nds) during this period. The basis of the 14s fell from 43 to 32 (11/32nds) during the same period. Meanwhile, there was much more negative carry incurred by those who were short the 14s. A summary P/L of the two trades was as follows:

12s of '13

Coupon Interest Paid	($9184.14)
Reverse RP Interest Earned	5644.29
Cash and Futures P/L	6750.00
Total	3210.15

14s of '11

Coupon Interest Paid	($10739.72)
Reverse RP Interest Earned	2525.63
Cash and Futures P/L	3437.50
Total	($4776.59)

The short sale of the 12s of '13 basis was profitable. A short sale of the 14s of '11 basis would have been a loser because of the low "special" rate. The large amount of negative carry on the 14s was also a cause of the smaller decline in the 14s basis relative to that of the 12s.

Monitoring Risk
This example demonstrates the importance of carefully choosing the issue as a candidate for a basis short sale. Always consider how much of an issue is available to borrow and how actively it trades. Once a short sale is established, be careful to monitor any changes in these conditions.

RP Specials and the Cheapest to Deliver
The possibility of specials complicates somewhat the problem of identifying the cheapest to deliver. If all bonds were stock or general collateral, then the bond with the highest implied repo rate would be the cheapest to deliver. To be more precise, one should compare a bond's implied repo rate with its own RP rate. The bond with the largest difference between its implied repo rate and its reverse repo rate is the cheapest to deliver.

Term Financing Versus Overnight Financing

For a basis trade, the cash bond can be financed with either a term RP or a string of overnight RP's. Financing overnight offers two advantages:

- With a positively-sloped yield curve, a string of overnight RP's can be cheaper than financing with a term RP.
- A position financed overnight is easier to unwind than a position financed with a term RP.

The chief drawback to financing a long basis position overnight is the exposure to a shift in the slope of the yield curve from positive to negative.

The Basis of a Non-Cheap Bond

Trading the basis of a bond other than the cheapest to deliver—the basis of a non-cheap bond—poses an interesting problem for the basis trader. The basis of a non-cheap bond really combines two positions:

- a spread position in the non-cheap and cheapest to deliver and
- a position in the basis of the cheapest to deliver

If you are long the basis of a non-cheap bond you are effectively:

- long the non-cheap bond and short the cheapest to deliver (in a ratio that described below) and
- long the basis of the cheapest to deliver

The basis of the cheapest to deliver is not the problem. The basis trader's problem when dealing with non-cheap bonds stems from the spread between the non-cheap bonds and the cheapest to deliver bonds. Why would the trader want such a position? What is the goal of the trade?

The usual motivation for spreading one bond against another is to take advantage of a change in the yield spread between the two. If this is the motivation, a well-constructed spread trade combines the two bonds in a ratio that produces the same payoff for any given change in the yield spread, regardless of whether yields rise on average, fall on average, or stay about unchanged. By this standard, a well-constructed long basis position involving a non-cheap bond should have the following properties:

- The position will profit from any increase in the basis of the cheapest to deliver.
- Any decrease in the basis of the cheapest to deliver will cost the position.
- The position will profit from *any* decrease in the yield of the non-cheap bond relative to the yield of the cheapest to deliver no matter whether yields are generally rising, falling, or staying the same.
- Any increase in the yield of the non-cheap bond relative to the yield of the cheapest to deliver will cost the position.

A related property of such a position is that its value will be relatively independent of changes in the general level of yields.

The conventional basis of a non-cheap bond does not have these properties. This section explains why a non-cheap bond's basis varies with the level of yields and shows how a "modified basis" position can be constructed to deal with the problem.

Bundled Trades

To see why a non-cheap bond's basis combines a bond spread with the basis of the cheapest to deliver, start with the basis of the non-cheap bond. By definition, the basis of a non-cheap bond is

$$B_n = P_n - C_n \times F$$

where

P_n is   the price of the non-cheap bond
C_n is   the conversion factor of the non-cheap bond
F is   the futures price

With a small amount of algebraic legerdemain, we can rewrite the basis of the non-cheap bond as:

$$B_n = [P_n - (C_n/C_c) \times P_c] + (C_n/C_c)[P_c - C_c \times F]$$

which is:

= [adjusted price difference between the non-cheap and the cheapest
to deliver bonds]

+

(C_n/C_c) [Basis of the cheapest to deliver]

where P_c and C_c represent the price and conversion factor of the cheapest to deliver. Satisfy yourself before we press on that this more complicated way of expressing the basis of the non-cheap bond simplifies to $[P_n - C_n \times F]$, which is what we started with.

The advantage of looking at the basis of a non-cheap bond this way is that you can see exactly what you've got. The basis of a non-cheap bond comprises

- a bond spread between the non-cheap and cheapest to deliver bonds in which the number of cheapest to deliver bonds for each non-cheap bond is given by the ratio of conversion factors and
- the basis of the cheapest to deliver, scaled by the ratio of the two bonds' conversion factors

Of the two, the one that poses the problem is the bond spread.

Bond Spread

The bond spread built into the non-cheap basis is short (C_n/C_c) market value of the cheapest to deliver for each dollar held long in the non-cheap bond. On the face of it, this arrangement makes a certain amount of sense. Suppose the non-cheap bond carries a low coupon while the cheapest to deliver bond carries a high coupon. The low-coupon bond would probably trade at a lower price than the high-coupon bond. Further, the price of the low-coupon bond would probably be less sensitive to a change in yields than would the price of the high-coupon bond. Thus, if one wanted to bet on a change in the yield spread between the two bonds, one would want to scale down the size of the position in the cheapest to deliver (say, the 10-3/8s of '12) to match the effective size of the position in the non-cheap bond (say, the 7-1/4s).

Is the ratio of conversion factors the right way to ratio the two bonds? If we compare the price responsiveness of the two bonds to equal changes in yields with the bonds' conversion factors, we find that the answer is *no*. A bond's conversion factor need not be proportional to its price sensitivity to a change in yields. As a result, the value of a bond spread constructed with the bonds' conversion factors will change with changes in the level of yields even if there is no change in the yield spread between the two bonds.

Consider, for example, a bond spread between the 7-1/4s of '16, which were a non-cheap bond on February 19, 1988, and the 10-3/8s of '12, which were the cheapest to deliver. Table 4.1 shows that a 1/32nd change in the price of the 10-3/8s results in a 0.297-basis-point change (in the opposite direction) in the bond's yield. Thus, a 10-basis-point increase in the yield of the 10-3/8s would cause the bond's price to fall 33.7/32nds (= 10 basis points/0.297). The same 10-basis-point increase in the yield of the 7-1/4s would cause the price of that bond to fall by 30.3/32nds (= 10 basis points/0.330).

Using these results, to spread the 7-1/4s against the 10-3/8s in a way that would be insensitive to equal changes in the yields of the two bonds, we would want to be short (30.3/33.7), or about 0.90, of the 10-3/8s for each dollar of the 7-1/4s held long.

Compare this ratio with the result of using the bonds' conversion factors. The conversion factor of the 7-1/4s was 0.9167, while the conversion factor of the 10-3/8s was 1.2326. Thus, we would be short (0.9167/1.2326), or about 0.74, of the 10-3/8s for each dollar of the 7-1/4s held long. We would be short too little of the 10-3/8s for a spread that should be insulated from changes in the general level of yields. In fact, this particular spread would be long the market. A decrease in yields would cause the value of the 7-1/4s held long in the position to go up more than the value of the 10-3/8s held short. Conversely, a rise in yields would cost the position money.

Table 4.1 Background Data for Calculating Hedge Ratios (February 19, 1988)

ISSUE	PRICE	YIELD	BASIS	CONVERSION FACTOR	YIELD VALUE OF 1/32nd	DOLLAR VALUE OF A BASIS POINT
10-3/8s of 11/15/12-07	116.02	8.66	19	1.2326	.00297	105.37
7-1/4s of 5/15/16	86.24	8.49	28	.9167	.00330	94.72
Futures	93.22	-		-	-	-

Table 4.2 Comparing Alternative Hedge Ratios

		PRICES AND YIELDS ON 10/16/87				HEDGE RATIOS		10/23/87			H.R. x CHANGE IN FUTURES PRICE		ERROR		DIFFERENCE
COUPON	MATURITY	CASH PRICE	YIELD	yv32	BASIS	C.F	CHG. yv32	YLD.	CHG. PR. (32nds)	FUT	C.F.	CHG. YV32	C.F.	YV32	
7.250	05/15/16-16	72.15	10.241	0.00440	19	0.9163	0.9163	-1.002	244	254	232.740	232.740	11.260	11.260	0
7.500	11/15/16-16	74.21	10.246	0.00431	20	0.9439	0.9354	-1.003	251	254	239.751	237.592	11.249	13.408	-2.159
8.750	05/15/17-17	86.14	10.210	0.00380	45	1.0841	1.0610	-1.016	290	254	275.361	269.494	14.639	20.506	-5.8674
9.250	02/15/16-16	90.27	10.244	0.00370	48	1.1389	1.0897	-1.021	301	254	289.281	276.784	11.719	24.216	-12.4968
8.875	08/15/17-17	87.27	10.177	0.00378	54	1.0996	1.0666	-1.025	298	254	279.044	270.916	18.956	27.084	-8.128
8.875	11/15/15-15	96.15	10.259	0.00351	56	1.2076	1.1486	-1.016	314	254	306.730	291.744	7.270	22.256	-14.986
10.375	11/15/12-07	99.28	10.387	0.00351	100	1.2336	1.1486	-0.974	279	254	313.334	291.744	-34.334	-12.744	-21.59
8.750	11/15/08-03	86.24	10.300	0.00410	100	1.0663	0.9833	-1.016	267	254	270.840	249.758	-3.840	17.242	-21.082
9.125	05/15/09-04	89.21	10.329	0.00400	105	1.1011	1.0079	-1.022	277	254	279.679	256.007	-2.679	20.993	-23.6728
11.250	02/15/15-15	109.25	10.180	0.00318	106	1.3574	1.2678	-0.972	335	254	344.780	322.021	-9.780	12.979	-22.7584
10.625	08/15/15-15	104.16	10.135	0.00325	106	1.2902	1.2405	-0.951	316	254	327.711	315.087	-11.711	0.913	-12.6238
9.375	02/15/06-06	92.16	10.289	0.00399	124	1.1300	1.0105	-1.056	279	254	287.020	256.667	-8.020	22.333	-30.353
12.500	08/15/14-09	118.20	10.331	0.00317	136	1.4583	1.2718	-0.995	339	254	370.408	323.037	-31.408	15.963	-47.371
11.750	11/15/14-09	112.26	10.270	0.00327	138	1.3833	1.2329	-0.876	286	254	351.358	313.157	-65.358	-27.157	-38.2016
12.000	08/15/13-08	114.08	10.319	0.00331	142	1.3999	1.2180	-0.968	314	254	355.575	309.372	-41.575	4.628	-46.2026
13.250	05/15/14-09	124.23	10.360	0.00302	146	1.5320	1.3350	-1.015	359	254	389.128	339.090	-30.128	19.910	-50.038
10.750	08/15/05-05	103.09	10.339	0.00379	151	1.2566	1.0638	-0.989	279	254	319.176	270.205	-40.176	8.795	-48.9712
12.750	11/15/10-05	119.18	10.335	0.00330	197	1.4459	1.2217	-1.001	319	254	367.259	310.312	-48.259	8.688	-56.9468
14.000	11/15/11-06	130.10	10.329	0.00302	211	1.5773	1.3350	-1.017	356	254	400.634	339.090	-44.634	16.910	-61.5442

AVERAGE	-12.905	9.921	-22.826
|AVERAGE|	23.526	16.210	27.631
S.D.	17.515	7.135	18.946

As a result, if the purpose of the bond spread is to profit from a fall in the yield of the 7-1/4s relative to the yield of the 10-3/8s, a spread constructed with conversion factors has the following flaw. Even if the yields move as predicted, the position could lose money if the change in the yield spread takes place with both yields rising.

Modified Basis for Non-Cheap Bonds

A modified basis might be better for trades involving non-cheap bonds. Further, the modified basis should take into account the price responsiveness of the non-cheap and cheapest to deliver bonds. To construct a modified basis for a non-cheap bond, we need to know how many futures to short for each $100,000 par value of the non-cheap bond. The appropriate ratio, given the simplifying assumption that the futures price tracks the price of the cheapest to deliver is as follows:

Hedge Ratio for Non-Cheap Bond

Conversion factor of the cheapest to deliver

multiplied by the

Yield value of a 32nd of the cheapest to deliver

divided by the

Yield value of a 32nd of the non-cheap bond

Given the value of the various parameters shown in Table 4.1, we find that the appropriate hedge ratio for the 7-1/4s should have been $1.11 = (1.2326 \times .00297/.00330)$. With this ratio, the gain on 1.11 short futures would have been 33.7/32nds (= $1.11 \times 30.3/32$nds), which would have just offset the fall in the price of the 7-1/4s.

If we use this hedge ratio, we find that the modified basis of the non-cheap bond can be written as:

$$MB_n = [P_n - (YV_c \times P_c] + (YV_c/YV_n)[P_c - C_c \times F],$$

which simplifies to:

$$MB_n = P_n - H_n \times F$$

There are two differences between this arrangement and what we had with the strictly-defined basis for the non-cheap bond—one important, the other less so. The important difference is that the bond spread is constructed the way it should be. Changes in the yield spread between the two bonds will pay off as predicted regardless of whether yields are rising, falling, or staying the same. The less important difference is that the position in the basis of the cheapest to deliver is scaled by the ratio of yield values of a 32nd rather than the by ratio of conversion factors. Because these are different ratios, the position in the cheapest to deliver's basis is different.

Importance of the Problem for Non-Cheap Bonds   The difference between a bond's hedge ratio and its conversion factor widens as the bond becomes more expensive to deliver. The bonds in Table 4.2 are ranked in order of cheapness to deliver, with the cheapest to deliver shown at the top. For bonds that are comparatively cheap to deliver, the difference between a strictly defined basis position and a modified basis position is comparatively small. For bonds that are fairly expensive to deliver, the differences can be substantial.

Implications for Basis Traders   The natural question is what basis traders should do with this information. The answer depends mainly on what the basis trader wants. The advantages of the modified basis trade for non-cheap bonds are clear. The most important disadvantage is that basis calculations are done with conversion factors, not with hedge ratios. As a result, a modified basis position could well stand still while the basis of the bond is rising.

The basis trader must choose, then, between two kinds of trades:

- the conventional basis trade that pays off in lockstep with changes in the basis but that is exposed to changes in the general level of yields

- the modified basis trade whose payoff is less closely tied to changes in the basis but that is insulated from changes in the general level of yields

Each has its advantages and disadvantages, and only the individual trader can decide which trade is the more desirable.

Implications for Hedgers For hedgers, the implications are straightforward. To the extent the futures price tracks the price of the cheapest to deliver, the hedge ratio for the modified basis provides a more reliable hedge than does the conversion factor, especially for relatively expensive bonds.

Hedgers nevertheless face a number of practical problems of their own, and what we have learned about the basis of a non-cheap bond sheds considerable light on the problems and risks in managing a hedge. Four points in particular are worth noting:

- The yield value of a 32nd changes as the level of yields changes.
- The cheapest to deliver can change to a different issue that would, in turn, have a different conversion factor and a different yield value of a 32nd.

Taken together, these two imply that hedge ratios should be monitored constantly and adjusted when necessary.

- The basis of the cheapest to deliver can change.
- The yield spread between the non-cheap bond and the cheapest to deliver can change.

These two constitute what is usually called "basis risk."

Little can be done about changes in the yield spreads, but not all changes in the basis of the cheapest to deliver are random or unpredictable. We can draw on information from Chapter 3 to learn how to manage this aspect of the hedge.

Basis of the Cheapest to Deliver   Any change in the basis of the
cheapest to deliver can be broken into two parts—the part that is random and the part that is systematically related to a change in the level
of yields. Nothing can be done about the first part, but the hedger can
exercise a certain amount of control over the second.

The discussion in Chapter 3 of shifting deliverables showed that the
cheapest to deliver is systematically related to the level of yields.
Suppose the three leading contenders for cheapest to deliver are the
12-3/4s of 11/10-05 (at low yields), the 10-3/8s of 11/12-07 (at yields
around 8 percent), and the 7-1/4s of 5/16 (at high yields). (See Table
2.2.)

Chart 4.1 shows the relationship between the bases of these three
bonds and the level of yields. The basis of the 12-3/4s flattens out as
yields fall. A rise in yields, however, causes the basis of the 12-3/4s to
rise. Moreover, the rise in the basis accelerates as yields rise, while the
fall in the basis decelerates as yields fall. If the hedger calculates the
hedge ratio using the method described above, an increase in yields
will produce a gain while a decrease in yields will produce a loss.
Moreover, the gain will be larger than the loss for the same basis point
change in yields. The hedger can balance the gains and losses by shorting a slightly smaller number of futures. The advantage of lightening
the hedge would be lower transaction costs. The disadvantage would
be the loss of the disproportionately large gain if yields rise.

Similarly, if the hedger is working in a high-yield setting, the hedged
position will tend to make money if yields fall and lose money if yields
rise. In this case, the hedge can be balanced by using slightly more futures than the yield value of a 32nd method dictates, but the disproportionately large gain if yields fall would be lost.

In the intermediate-yield range, the basis can rise whichever way
yields go, at least until there is a shift in the cheapest to deliver. Ad-
justing the hedge to compensate for these changes, however, would
probably do little good. There are enough problems and uncertainties
in cash/futures price relationships that dealing with the change in the
basis most likely would be overkill.

Chart 4.1   Basis versus Yield

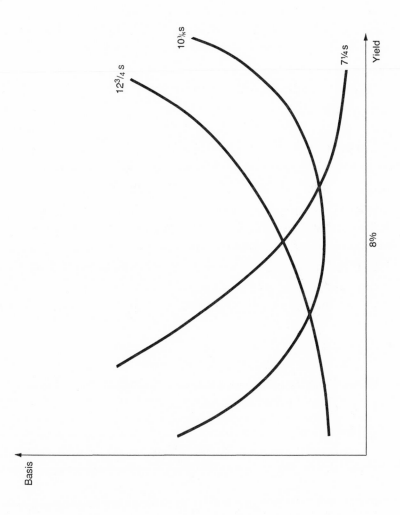

Basis

Yield

$12^3/_4$ s

$10^3/_8$ s

$7^1/_4$ s

8%

Relation of Futures Price to Cheapest to Deliver   Considerable attention has been devoted so far to the problem of shifting deliverables.
One implication not drawn from such shifts is the effect they have on
the behavior of the futures price.

When there is comparatively little uncertainty about what the
cheapest to deliver will be, there is also comparatively little question
about how the futures price will behave. It will track the price of the
cheapest to deliver.

How should the futures price behave when two bonds are equally
cheap? Chart 4.1 shows that if yields were in the neighborhood of 9
percent, the 7-1/4s and the 10-3/8s would be more-or-less equally
cheap to deliver. Which should the futures track? The correct theoretical answer is that the futures should reflect the possibility that either
bond could be the cheapest to deliver and, perhaps, track a weighted
average of the two bonds' prices. The weights in such an exercise might
be the probabilities that the market attaches to the likelihood that each
bond will be the cheapest to deliver.

In practice, how the futures price behaves in these gray areas is an
empirical matter, and the hedger should be willing to do the empirical
work required to stay on top of this relationship as it evolves over time.

Short Squeeze

Trading the basis from the short side (selling cash bonds short and
buying futures) involves several risks that must be considered:

- The proceeds from the short sale must be invested in a reverse
  repo, and the particular issue sold short must be "reversed in." The
  reverse repo rate for readily-available collateral is generally 25 to
  100 basis points lower than the repo rate.
- If the issue is not readily available to reverse in, you only earn the
  reverse repo "special" rate. There is no theoretical limit to how
  low the special rate can go. It can even go negative in extreme circumstances.

- The short seller of a cash bond must pay the coupon interest until the short sale is covered. This expense is most often greater than the interest earned on the reverse repo. (In such a case, the short seller's carry is negative.)
- The short seller is obligated eventually to buy back the same issue that was sold short. This can become difficult with illiquid issues, or with any issue that is involved in a "short squeeze."

A *short squeeze* develops when the obligations of short sellers to cover their sales greatly exceed the amount of an issue that is readily available. The most obviously attractive basis short sales often pose the greatest danger of being hurt by a short squeeze. This is due to the increased demand to reverse in the issue and to buy it back when many basis traders are selling the same issue.

Short Squeeze of 1986

The most dramatic basis short squeeze in recent memory was the 9-1/4 of '16 short squeeze in May 1986. In April, the 9-1/4s of '16 were trading at a yield spread of between 25 to 40 basis points below the 12s of '13, which was one of the cheapest bonds to deliver. During May, the yield spread rose to over 100 basis points. This caused the 9-1/4 basis to widen by about 6 points, or $60,000 per $1 million face value. Meanwhile, the basis of the high-coupon, shorter-maturity bonds, such as the 12s of '13, continued to narrow and approach convergence. Chart 4.2 shows the contrast between the move in the 9-1/4 basis and the move in the 12 basis during this period.

What Caused the Short Squeeze? This dramatic short squeeze was caused by the following factors:

- It seemed like an obvious spread play to short the outstanding current long bond (the 9-1/4s) against a long position in the new "when issued" long bond, which was the old 9-7/8s of '15, the futures contract, or a yield curve play against the 10-year note. During several earlier cycles, the current bond had traded at a

Chart 4.2 September 1986 Bond Basis (Period: 1/1/86 to 9/19/86)

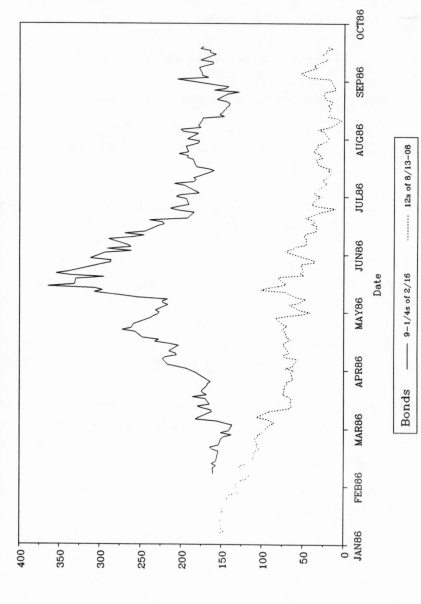

Source: DCNYF Research Group

premium to other bonds and had given up the premium after the refunding when it was replaced by a new current bond. Expecting a similar pattern, spreaders built up a massive short position in the 9-1/4s.

- Most of the 9-1/4 issue was owned by Japanese institutions that did not make the issue available to borrow in the repo market. There was no theoretical problem here. Rather, Japanese institutions were unaccustomed to RP transactions and were unwilling to set what for them would have been a precedent. Nevertheless, the effect was staggering. The RP spread rate on the 9-1/4s approached 0 percent, and finally the issue couldn't be borrowed at all. There were rumors that some small dealers had traded the issue at a negative reverse RP rate. This means that they paid interest to lend money for the privilege of reversing in the 9-1/4s as collateral.
- The problem was compounded by funds selling old issues that were approaching historical cost because of the decline in yields. Many of these older issues were cheap to deliver, and having them sold out of portfolio only caused the basis of the 9-1/4s to widen further.

The short squeeze of the 9-1/4s occurred with a rare combination of events. The market was unusually disorderly. It seems unlikely that things could ever be that bad again.

Controlling the Risk of Short Squeeze

To minimize the risk of a short squeeze in a basis short sale, the trader must:

- Choose an issue that is available to borrow and to buy back to cover the short. Check the reverse RP rate (both overnight and term), and the issue size (see quote sheet).
- Monitor carefully for signs of the possible development of a short squeeze. Three main signs of a short squeeze are:

- a declining RP special rate
- a large amount of short sales in an issue
- changes in its yield spread to similar issues

• Consider using a stop-loss point to establish a maximum risk level. Theoretically, there is no maximum limit to a potential loss on a basis short sale when the bond you are short is being squeezed.

Basis Short Sales vs. Selling the Basis Out of Portfolio

In principle, the risks of a short squeeze are the same whether the basis sale is accomplished by selling the bonds short or by selling the bonds out of a portfolio. In the first case, however, any losses from a short squeeze take the form of hard cash payments. In the second case, the loss takes the form of a foregone capital gain. The first is a *realized loss* while the second is an *opportunity loss*; both are equally real. However, the practical consequences of the realized loss, which takes the form of cash paid out, are more dire than those of the missed opportunity, which takes the form of a reduction in long-term performance.

The portfolio manager's comfort comes from not needing to recognize the loss. When it comes time to unwind the basis trade and put bonds back into the portfolio, the portfolio manager is not constrained to buy back the same bond that was sold in the first place. In the spring of 1986, for example, the 9-1/4s easily could have been replaced by a bond of similar maturity and coupon but with a substantially higher yield. Many active portfolio managers were swapping out of the 9-1/4s at the time anyway.

The good news is that the depressing effect of a short squeeze on the performance of a portfolio manger who sells the basis is offset at least in part by the gains from the basis sale. In fact, Chapter 8 shows that a portfolio manager who regularly sold the basis using a diversified portfolio of bonds would have outperformed the cash portfolio even with the dramatic short squeeze of 1986.

Taking a Basis Trade Into the Delivery Month

As the delivery month approaches, the prospect of either making or taking delivery becomes a real consideration. The first notice day falls on the second business day before the beginning of the contract month.

Some basis traders are better suited than others to make or take delivery. Those who would find delivery a costly undertaking have two main alternatives

- Unwind the trade with offsetting transactions
- Roll the futures leg of the trade over to the next contract month

Those who are short the basis have a third alternative: to "refresh" the long futures position. This is done by buying and selling futures in the same contract month. While this may seem a strange thing to do, the transactions get rid of old long positions and put new long positions in their place. Because deliveries are assigned to the oldest longs, the transactions allow the trader to forestall the possibility of taking delivery on a long futures position, at least until the last trading day. All open long positions after the last trading day must, of course, stand for delivery.

Even those for whom delivery is not especially costly must think about delivery as the last trading day approaches. The value of the basis of the cheapest to deliver at this point reflects the combined value of remaining carry and the value of the switch option. If the trader thinks the switch option is mispriced, the most attractive alternative may be to set up the position for delivery, buying or selling futures so that there is exactly one futures contract for each $100,000 par value of the bonds in the position.

Altogether, then, there are three main alternatives (not counting the refreshing trade):

- Unwind the trade
- Roll the futures
- Set up for delivery

Unwinding the Trade

Unwinding a trade involves taking offsetting positions in both the cash and futures market. Chapter 1 provides examples of how this is done for both long and short basis positions.

Rolling the Futures

Rolling the futures involves replacing the futures in the position with futures from the next contract month. For example, if you are long the basis and therefore short futures, rolling the futures means buying futures in the lead or current contract month and selling futures in the next contract month. The effect of these transactions is the same as simultaneously selling the basis in the current month and buying the basis in the next contract month.

If you are short the basis, rolling the futures requires selling futures in the lead contract month and buying futures in the next contract month. In this case, rolling the futures means that you simultaneously buy the current month basis and sell the basis in the next contract month.

When you roll the futures, therefore, you eliminate any concerns about deliveries in the current month. For example, if you were short the basis, you no longer need be concerned about wild card deliveries. At the same time, you are taking a new view on a new basis. Whether this is a reasonable thing to do depends largely on how you view the futures calendar spread.

For the most part, the spread between futures prices for the lead month and any deferred month changes very little. Occasionally, however, when trading activity begins to switch from the lead contract into the next contract, the futures price spread changes temporarily and briefly opens a window during which rolling the basis trade forward by rolling the futures can make sense.

In practice, rolling the futures entails nothing more than "buying the futures calendar spread" or "selling the futures calendar spread." Buying the futures calandar spread means buying the front month contract and selling the back month contract. Selling the spread is just the opposite. To roll over long basis positions, one buys the futures spread. One sells the spread to roll over short basis positions.

Recall that a bond's conversion factor is the approximate price at which the bond would yield 8 percent to maturity or first call as of the first delivery day of the contract month. The only thing that can complicate an otherwise simple trade is that the conversion factors are different for each contract month. Because the bond will have three fewer months remaining to maturity by the time the first day of the next contract month rolls around, the conversion factor will be closer to one.

As a practical matter, however, the difference is quite small and matters only for large basis positions, usually over $100 million. For example, the March 1988 conversion factor for the 10-3/8s of 11/12-07 was 1.2326 while its June 1988 conversion factor was 1.2310. In a basis trade involving $10 million par value of the bonds, the trader would be long or short 123 futures irrespective of the contract month. In a basis trade involving $100 million, on the other hand, the March 1988 basis trade would call for 1,233 futures while the June '88 basis trade would call for 1,231 futures. The difference is small but gets larger with the size of the trade and the number of times the trade is rolled.

Setting Up for Delivery

Carrying the trade through delivery means simply accepting delivery for short basis positions, or making delivery for long basis positions.

The key to setting up for delivery is "covering the tail." Each futures contract calls for the delivery of $100,000 par value of an eligible bond. A well-hedged basis trade, however, requires doing futures in a ratio to cash. In the case of the 10-3/8s of 11/12-07, for example, the ratio of futures to bonds in the position would be 1.23 futures for each $100,000 par value of the bonds if they were the cheapest to deliver. This would be 123 futures for each $10 million face value of the bonds. (If the 10-3/8s were not the cheapest to deliver, a different ratio might be appropriate for the reasons laid out earlier in this chapter.)

Once trading in the expiring futures contract stops on the last day of trading, however, the correct ratio of futures to bonds for a well-hedged position is one-to-one. The extra 23 futures contracts in the basis trade with the 10-3/8s represent unwanted price risk. For example, if you are long $10 million of the 10-3/8s and short 100 futures contracts, you are completely hedged. You know the invoice price at which you can sell each of the bonds.

If you keep the extra 23 short futures after the expiration of trading in the futures, however, you are exposed to an increase in bond prices. You must make delivery on the 23 futures, and if bond prices rise, you will lose the difference between the converted futures price, which is fixed when trading stops and the higher cash price of the bond.

You can "cover the tail" in the trade either by reducing the short futures position by 23 contracts or by adding $2.3 million to the size of the cash position. In either case, the trick to covering the tail is to do it as close in time as possible to the termination of futures trading. Any mismatch in timing exposes you to price risk. At the same time, trading at the closing bell can be tumultuous and takes place within a range of prices. The best time to cover the tail in a basis trade, therefore, is just before the close of trading. The timing mismatch that results is small and the market typically is liquid.

Chapter 5

How the Basis Has Behaved Since 1977

Our understanding of what drives bond futures and of the options that are embedded in the contract terms did not emerge fully formed on the day the bond futures pit was first opened for trading. For that matter, when it was first introduced in 1977, the bond futures contract was thought to be too complicated, and there was some question about whether it would succeed. The "delivered basket" idea, which was old hat in conventional commodity futures, was new to financial futures, and the markets took some time to adjust.

As it turned out, the years since 1977 have been exceptionally fruitful for learning the ins and outs of the futures contract. The Treasury securities market has covered a lot of ground over the past 11 years. Yields have gone from comparatively low levels in the 1970s to what were, by U.S. standards, phenomenally high levels in the early 1980s. The slope of the yield curve has gone from positive, to negative, and back to positive again twice. Yields have gone from being stable, to highly volatile, to comparatively stable, and back to comparatively volatile.

Each radical change in the interest-rate environment, whether in the level of yields, the slope of the yield curve, or the overall volatility of yields, has brought to light a new facet of the relationship between the futures contract and the market for Treasury securities.

This chapter chronicles these events and how they shaped our understanding of the futures contract and the embedded options discussed in Chapters 2 and 3. The real purpose of this chapter is to impart an appreciation to the reader for how bond futures have responded to new interest-rate environments. We have many more configurations of interest-rate levels and volatilities left to experience, and we can best prepare for these new settings by understanding how the futures have responded to new situations in the past.

Volatility of Yields since 1977

Paul Volcker arrived at the Fed when inflation in the United States was running out of control. By the fall of 1979, the situation had become intolerable and Volcker's Fed embarked on a period of sharply tighter money.

The effect of those policies and their aftermath is best characterized by the three panels of Chart 5.1. The top panel shows what has happened to the level of yields, as measured by yields on 20-year Treasury bonds. When Volcker began his term, long-term rates were around 8 percent. Before long, long-term rates rose to the neighborhood of 14 percent, a level from which yields have been falling on and off ever since.

The second panel shows what happened to the slope of the yield curve, which we measure by the difference between the yield on 20-year Treasury bonds and 3-month Treasury bills. The initial impact of tight money was to force short-term yields well above long-term yields. This was followed by the "free fall" of short-term rates during the spring of 1980, which in turn was followed by a second sortie into negative-yield curve territory. Since late 1981, the slope of the yield curve has been "normal" (i.e., positive).

The bottom panel shows the volatility of long-term Treasury yields. The change in monetary policy regimes prompted a sharp increase in yield volatility. Since then, following a brief settling down in 1984, bond yields have been more volatile than they were in the 1970s, though not quite as volatile as they were during the early Volcker years.

Chart 5.1

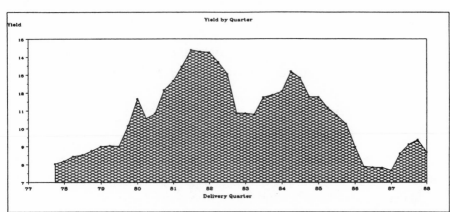

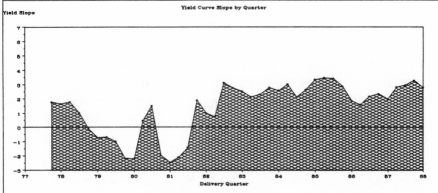

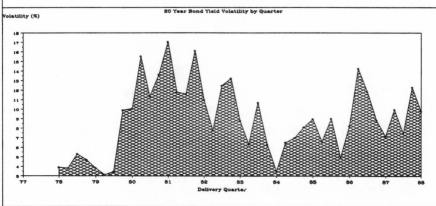

Throughout these dramatic shifts in yield-curve settings, the behavior of the bond futures contract has gone through four more-or-less distinct periods:

- Cash and carry— 1977 to the first quarter of 1979
- Negative yield curve—first quarter of 1979 through the end of 1981
- Positive yield curve—1982 to the end of 1984
- Short basis—1985 to the present

This chapter presents the characteristics of each of these periods in turn, tracking the record of actual bond deliveries at the Chicago Board of Trade as a guide to T-bond futures behavior.

Cash and Carry Period: 1977–First Quarter 1979

This period is perhaps the easiest to describe. Yields were low and stable, and the yield curve was positively sloped (see Chart 5.2). These were the early days of the bond contract and its trading was very similar to other contracts (i.e., wheat, corn, and soy beans traded at the Board of Trade). Bonds were bought in the cash market and sold in the futures market if the cost of financing those bonds for the period was less than the price differential between the bonds and the futures. Nothing could have been simpler.

With the positively-sloped yield curve, it paid to buy bonds and deliver them against the futures. Moreover, it paid to deliver them on the last possible day. The top panel of Chart 5.3 bears this out, showing in the form of an index the average delivery date of delivered bonds. The index is constructed so that a bond delivered on the first day of the delivery month has a delivery index reading of one; a bond delivered on the last day has an index of reading of 30. For most of this period, the delivery index is close to 30, which indicates that all or nearly all bonds were delivered on the last possible day.

The average factor of delivered bonds is shown in the middle panel of Chart 5.3. Yields were about 8 percent, and the range of coupons for

Chart 5.2

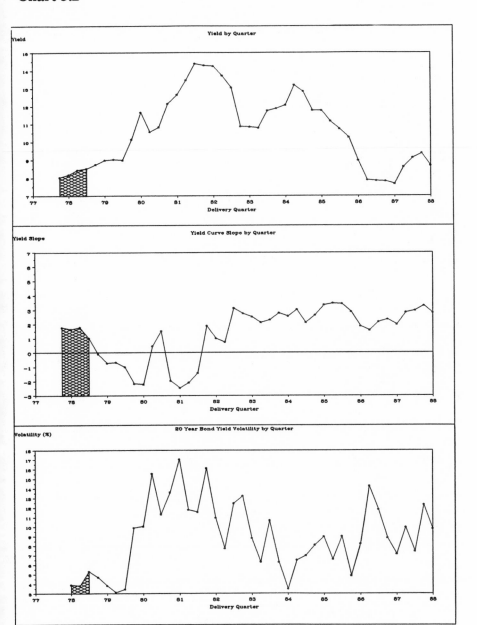

Chart 5.3

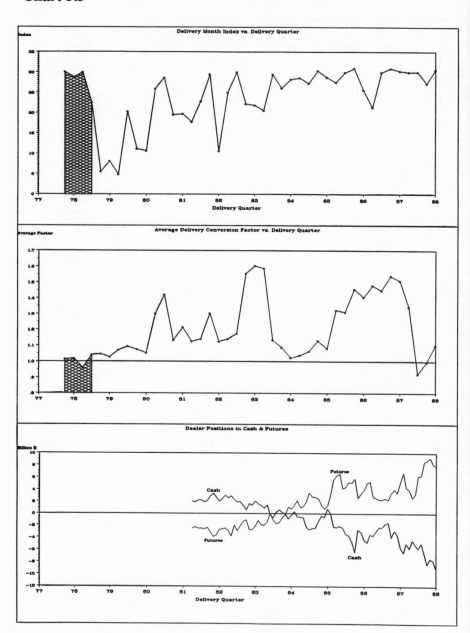

deliverable issues was comparatively narrow. As a result, the average factor of delivered bonds was close to one.

By the end of 1978, deliveries began to come in early. It was at this time that the bond futures contract began to change character and that some of the richness of the contract began to come to light.

Negative Yield Curve Period: First Quarter 1979–1981

This was the era when Paul Volcker was conducting his monetarist experiment. Its consequences for interest rates are demonstrated vividly in the three panels of Chart 5.4, which highlights the yields, yield curve slope, and yield volatility during this era. Yields rose from 8-1/2 to 14-1/2 percent. The slope of the yield curve swung back and forth between negative and positive; at times, short-term rates exceeded long-term rates by as much as 200 basis points. The period is also characterized by sharply rising yield volatility. Volatility rose from a sleepy 4 percent (annualized) to well over 16 percent.

The effect of this environment on the bond futures contract is fascinating. The most obvious consequence of a negatively-sloped yield curve is that it costs money to hold bonds for a long time. Therefore, one would expect bond deliveries to take place early in the delivery month. This is borne out by the top panel of Chart 5.5, which shows that most deliveries took place within the first week of the delivery month, at least during the first few delivery cycles.

Then a curious thing happened. The yield curve slope became even more negative, but deliveries started taking place later and later rather than earlier and earlier.

The explanation for this delivery behavior is rooted in the "wild card" option. As described in Chapter 3, a wild card play is the delivery of bonds into the futures market in response to a sharp change in bond prices after futures trading has stopped for the day. To take advantage of the wild card, at least three things are required:

Chart 5.4

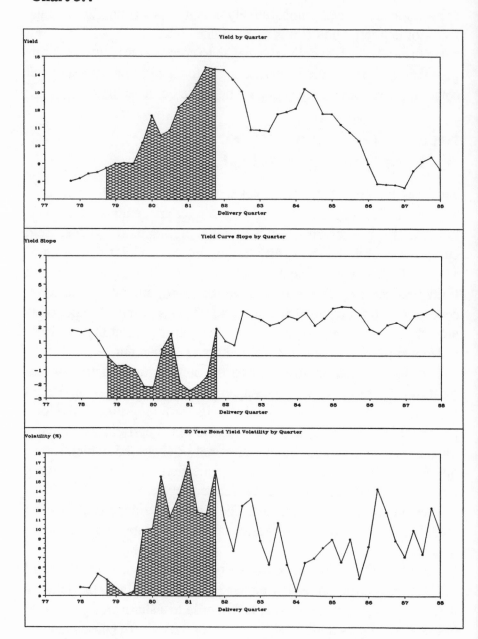

- A short position in bond futures
- A delivery factor of the delivered bond significantly different from one
- Volatility of bonds enough to cause a big change in bond prices between the close of the futures market and the close of the cash market

Of these three, the second two were ushered in with the new interest-rate regime. The high level of yields brought with them high-coupon Treasury bonds, which in turn carried the high conversion factors needed to make the wild card play profitable. Notice that the average factor of delivered bonds reached 1.4 during this era. Moreover, the high volatility of yields, especially in late-afternoon trading when the money supply figures were released, provided the necessary swings in bond prices.

Thus, the wild card option gained value (the top panel of Chart 5.5 shows its effect on deliveries). Even though carry was negative during much of this period, traders were holding onto their short futures positions to take advantage of wild card opportunities. As they did, deliveries tended to fall later and later in the contract month.

The bottom panel of Chart 5.5 reveals another phenomenon. At the beginning of 1981, the Federal Reserve began to require primary government securities dealers to report their positions in both cash bonds and futures. These figures are made available to the public with about a month lag by the Federal Reserve. The bottom panel of Chart 5.5 shows that dealers were, on balance, long cash bonds and short a roughly equivalent number of bond futures. That is, they were "long the basis."

Positive Carry Period: 1982–1984

Starting in 1982, yields began to decline, and the yield curve resumed its "normal," or positive, slope. Volatility fell off somewhat from its

Chart 5.5

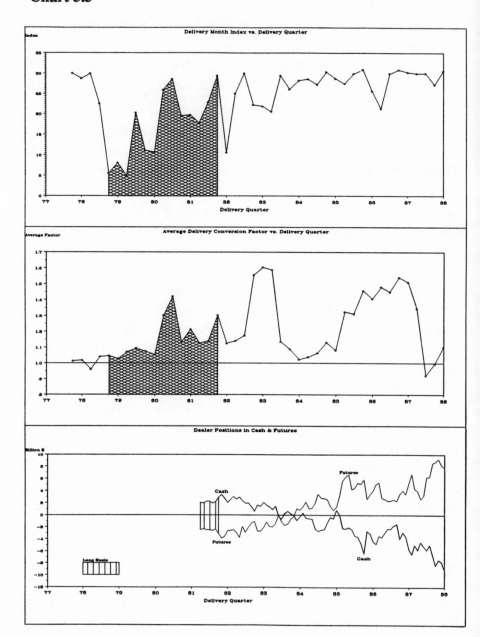

highs in the early 1980s, and actually returned to its old levels briefly in 1984. Chart 5.6 shows these features of the interest-rate market.

With the return of positive carry, there was no longer a clear cost incentive to deliver bonds early. Rather, the incentive is to deliver as late in the contract month as possible. The delivery evidence bears this out. The top panel of Chart 5.7 shows that most bonds were delivered near the end of the contract month.

The exceptions to this rule took place during the second half of 1982 and the first quarter of 1983 when the average delivery factor was close to 20 days. A wild card option was at work. In this case, however, carry was positive and the effect of the wild card was to accelerate rather than delay deliveries. The presence of wild card plays during these delivery cycles is evident in the average conversion factor of the delivered bonds, which reached 1.6.

The bottom panel of Chart 5.7 reveals that dealers stayed long the basis until the middle of this period so that they too could take advantage of the shorts' wild card option. From the middle of 1983, however, the primary dealers positions began to shift to a short basis. As yields stabilized, the volatility requirement for wild card plays disappeared. Factors of the cheapest bonds being delivered moved back to the neighborhood of 1.0.

Short Basis Period: 1985–Second Quarter 1988

The final period in this chronicle runs from the first quarter of 1985 to the present (summer 1988). Chart 5.8 shows that yields were generally falling, the yield curve was comparatively flat but still positively sloped, and yields were fairly volatile.

This period does not appear much different from the preceding one; Chart 5.9 shows that most deliveries took place at the end of the delivery month. Some wild card options were exercised early in 1986, and a possible switch option in late 1987.

Chart 5.6

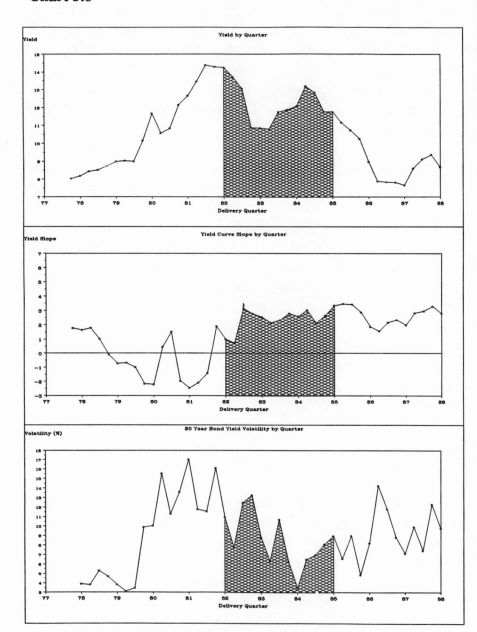

Chart 5.7

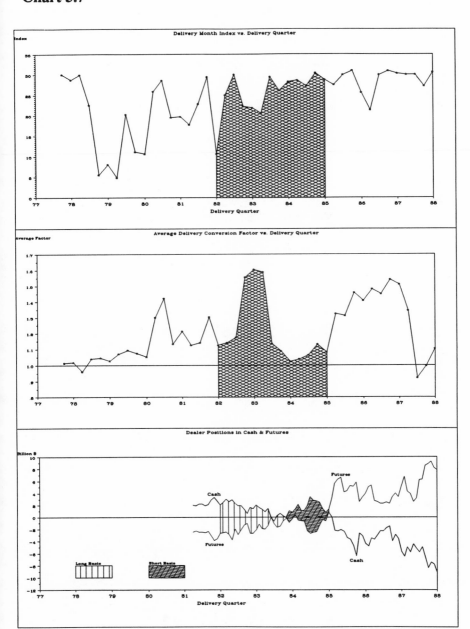

Chart 5.8

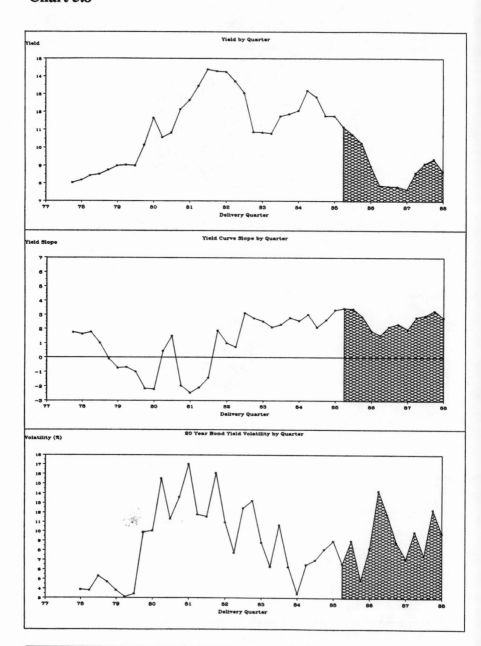

Chart 5.9

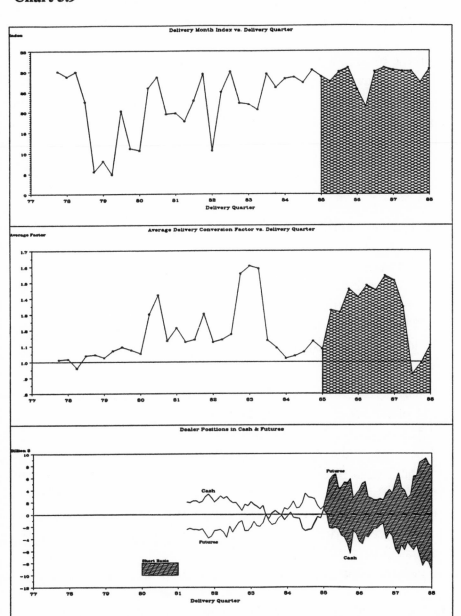

Even so, the positions of primary government securities dealers suggest that something about the period was different. Note that dealers throughout these years have been short the basis, and they have been short the basis in a positive carry environment.

Their behavior cannot be explained by the change in the yield curve as a whole. The shift in their basis position seems to have been prompted in the first instance by a change in the slope of the long end of the yield curve.

Around 1985, a number of events conspired to cause great demand for long-dated Treasury bonds.

- The bull market in bonds caused demand for long-dated zero-coupon bonds.
- The U.S. Treasury, in an effort to accommodate this demand, stopped issuing callable bonds and 20-year bonds, and concentrated on fixed maturity 30-year bonds.
- The reserve surplus of Japan began to be invested aggressively in long-dated Treasury bonds.

Chart 5.10A shows the effect of these events, the difference in the yield of the longest-maturity deliverable bond and the yield of the shortest-maturity deliverable bond.

The effect of the increase in demand for long-dated Treasury bonds is clear. The slope of the long end of the yield curve became sharply negative. By the middle of 1985, the longest eligible bonds yielded 30 basis points less than the shortest eligible bonds. They became extremely expensive, and dealers shorted the cash bonds and hedged by buying futures contracts. (See Chart 5.10B.)

Since then, the short basis position of the primary dealers has continued to grow, even though the relative expensiveness of long-dated Treasury bonds has fallen off for the most part. What accounts for the growth?

The dealers discovered the profitability of being short the basis as a byproduct of their initial yield-curve play with long-dated bonds. They found that the premium in the basis is too large and that the embedded options in short futures positions have been overpriced. As a result, a short basis position has, with one impressive interruption during the short squeeze of 1986, been a profitable position to maintain. Chapter 8 provides further evidence on this point, as it discusses applications of the basis for portfolio managers.

The switch option, which appeared on the scene after 1985, comes into play during the week or so remaining in the delivery month after trading in the futures contract has expired. The basic ingredients for the switch option to have value are these:

- Yield of 7 to 9 percent so that there are two or more close contenders for the cheapest to deliver
- Sufficient volatility in yields to create uncertainty in traders' minds about which bond might actually be cheapest to deliver

As yields passed through the 9-percent region, the first of these conditions was met. Further, there have been enough episodes of high yield-volatility during this era to supply the uncertainty. As a result, the switch option has had a noticeable influence on the bond basis during a number of futures expirations. The effect is not absolutely clear in the delivery evidence, however, largely because the switch option, even if exercised, does not accelerate deliveries.

Concluding Remarks

At the outset of trading in bond futures, no one could have anticipated that dealers would be short the basis in a negative yield-curve environment. Even so, this came about because of the relative pricing of short- and long-maturity deliverable bonds.

In the future, the relative pricing of bonds in a negative yield-curve environment might well lead to different patterns of behavior from those in the early 1980s. We have learned a great deal about the be-

Chart 5.10A Average Spread Between Long and Short Maturity Deliverable Bond Yield vs. Delivery Quarter

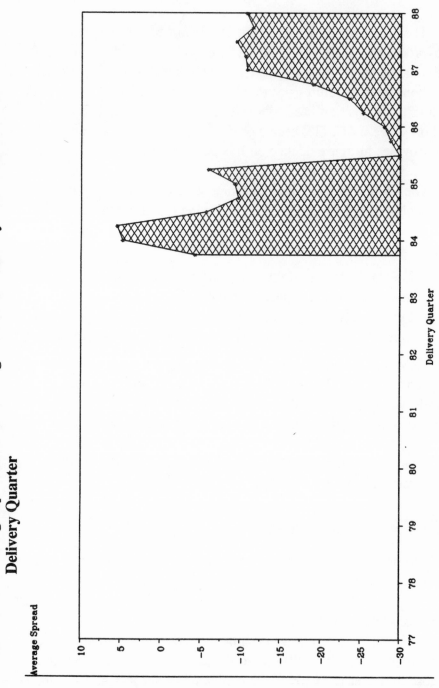

Average Spread

Delivery Quarter

Chart 5.10B Dealer Positions in Cash & Futures

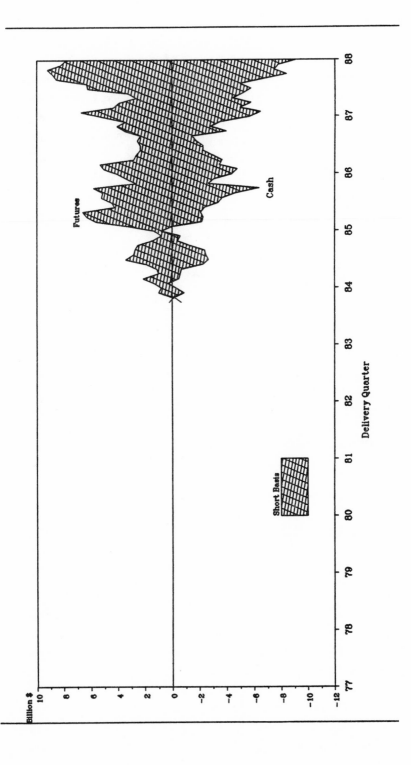

havior of the bond futures contract, but it would be presumptuous to suppose that we have seen and know it all. New and sophisticated players are coming into the Treasury market all the time. The economic and policy forces at play now are quite different from those in place several years ago. Our own prognosis is that the bond contract will continue its intriguing behavior well into the next decade.

Chapter 6

Quarterly Delivery Cycles in 1987

We first drafted the manuscript for this book in early 1988, when trading patterns from 1987 were still fresh in our minds. At the time, our intent in describing quarterly delivery cycles in considerable detail was to provide a chronicle of recent history. By the time we finished drafting the manuscript, the March and June 1988 delivery cycles had come and gone, and it became apparent that 1987 would be old hat by the time the book reached even the first reader.

We decided to keep the discussion in the final manuscript, however, largely because 1987 was so rich in real-life examples of the theoretical possibilities described in Chapters 1–4. For example, a number of shifts in the deliverable bond took place. The switch option was a noticeable factor at least once, although it expired worthless. Further, the bond market rally that followed the stock market crash of October 19, 1987, produced some sharp swings in the bases of the cheapest to deliver and non-cheap bonds. About the only thing that was missing was a wild card play, which we haven't seen in the U.S. in several years. All in all, one couldn't have found a better year for illustrating the practical side of trading the basis.

March 1987 Cycle

The 14s of 11/11 ended up the cheapest to deliver on the last trading day in March with a basis of 2/32nds. These were followed closely by the 12s of 8/13-08, which finished with a basis of 3/32nds. Table 6.1

shows that these bonds together with a number of other high-coupon, callable bonds dominated total deliveries.

The highlight of the March delivery cycle, however, was the comparatively rapid collapse of the bases of the 7-1/4s of 5/16 and the 7-1/2s of 11/16. (See Chart 6.1.) To a large extent, this represented the beginning of a recovery from the colossal short squeeze of the 9-1/4s by the Japanese in 1986.

Table 6.1   March 1987 Bond Deliveries

DATE (YYMMDD)	COUPON	MATURITY	NUMBER DELIVERED	FACTOR
870331	14.000	11/15/11-06	3484	1.5875
870331	12.750	11/15/10-05	2894	1.4546
870331	12.000	8/15/13-08	1293	1.4053
870331	13.875	5/15/11-06	1227	1.5689
870331	13.250	5/15/14-09	1212	1.5394
870331	11.750	11/15/14-09	2	1.3885
870331	12.500	8/15/14-09	2	1.4640
870330	12.750	11/15/10-05	1039	1.4546
870330	14.000	11/15/11-06	670	1.5875
870330	13.250	5/15/14-09	293	1.5394
870330	13.875	5/15/11-06	208	1.5689
870327	12.750	11/15/10-05	1400	1.4546
870327	14.000	11/15/11-06	581	1.5875
870327	13.875	5/15/11-06	120	1.5689
870326	12.750	11/15/10-05	1	1.4546
870326	14.000	11/15/11-06	1	1.5875
870325	12.750	11/15/10-05	1	1.4546
TotalDeliveries, Average Conversion Factor =			14428	1.5150

Source: Appendix I

June 1987 Cycle

The key points of the second quarter were the continued collapse of the basis of the 7-1/4s and the 7-1/2s and a shift in the cheapest to deliver.

Chart 6.1A Basis for March 1987 Deliverable Bonds

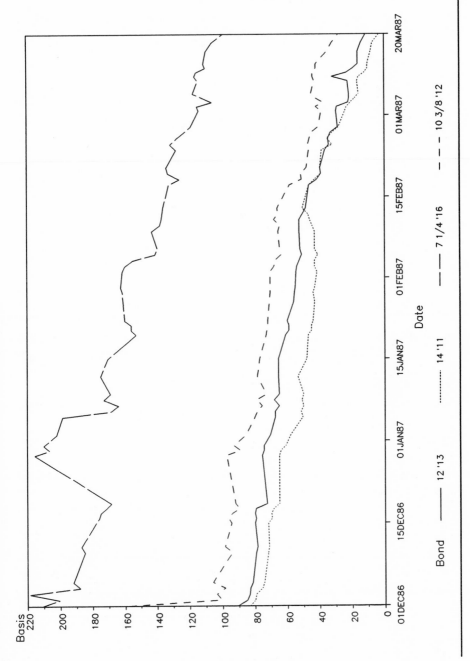

Basis
220

Bond ——— 12 '13   .... 14 '11   ——— 7 1/4 '16   – – 10 3/8 '12

Date

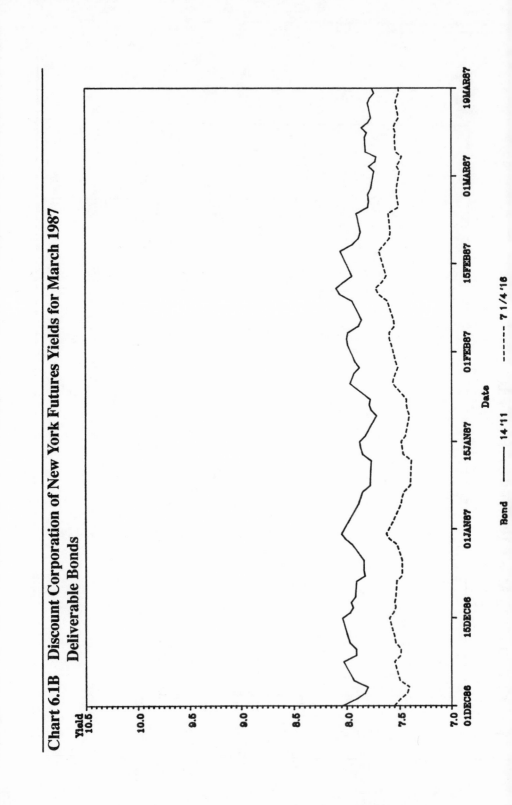

Chart 6.1B Discount Corporation of New York Futures Yields for March 1987
Deliverable Bonds

Chart 6.2 shows that the basis of the 7-1/4s, for example, fell from the neighborhood of 150/32nds to 27/32nds on the last day of trading. Corresponding to this continuing collapse was a further narrowing of the yield spreads between high- and low-coupon bonds.

Yields rose substantially during the quarter, and the 14s, which finished with a basis of 32/32nds on the last trading day, were replaced by the 13-1/4s of 5/14-09 and the 12-1/2s of 8/14-09, which finished with a basis of 12/32nds. (These were followed very closely by the 12s of 8/13-08, which had a basis of 13 on the last trading day.)

The size of the basis of the cheapest bonds to deliver on the last trading day is striking. But then, there was considerable uncertainty about where yields might go between the last trading day and the last delivery day. A big rally might have precipitated a shift in the cheapest to deliver to the 7-1/4s. Those who were long the futures faced a sizeable risk in the bonds they might receive. The wide basis on the last trading day reflects the value of the short's switch option and the compensation longs required to bear that risk. As it was, however, the 12s and 12-1/2s came in as the cheapest to deliver, and no switch option developed. Table 6.2 shows that total deliveries were dominated by the 12s.

Table 6.2   June 1987 Bond Deliveries

DATE (YYMMDD)	COUPON	MATURITY	NUMBER DELIVERED	FACTOR
870630	12.00	8/15/13-08	5913	1.4037
870630	12.50	8/15/24-09	900	1.4623
870626	7.25	5/15/16	5	0.9159
870625	12.00	8/15/13-08	5	1.4037
Total Deliveries, Average Conversion Factor = 6823				1.4111

Source: Appendix I

Chart 6.2A   Basis for June 1987 Deliverable Bonds

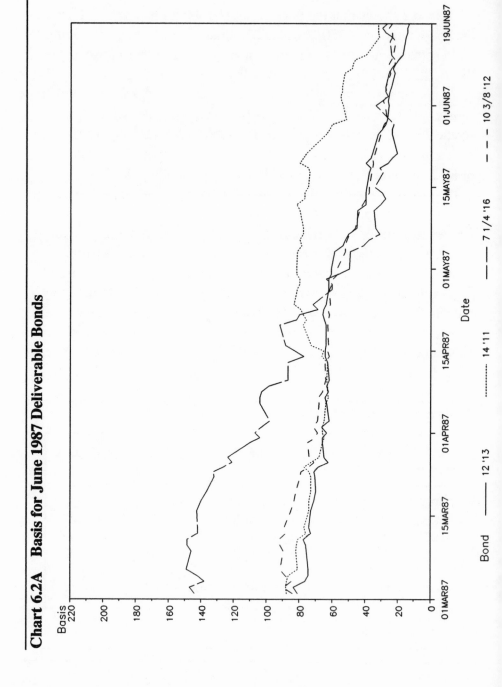

Basis

220
200
180
160
140
120
100
80
60
40
20
0

01MAR87   15MAR87   01APR87   15APR87   01MAY87   15MAY87   01JUN87   19JUN87

Date

Bond ———— 12 '13 ·········· 14 '11 ——— 7 1/4 '16 — — 10 3/8 '12

Chart 6.2B   Discount Corporation of New York Futures Yields for June 1987 Deliverable Bonds

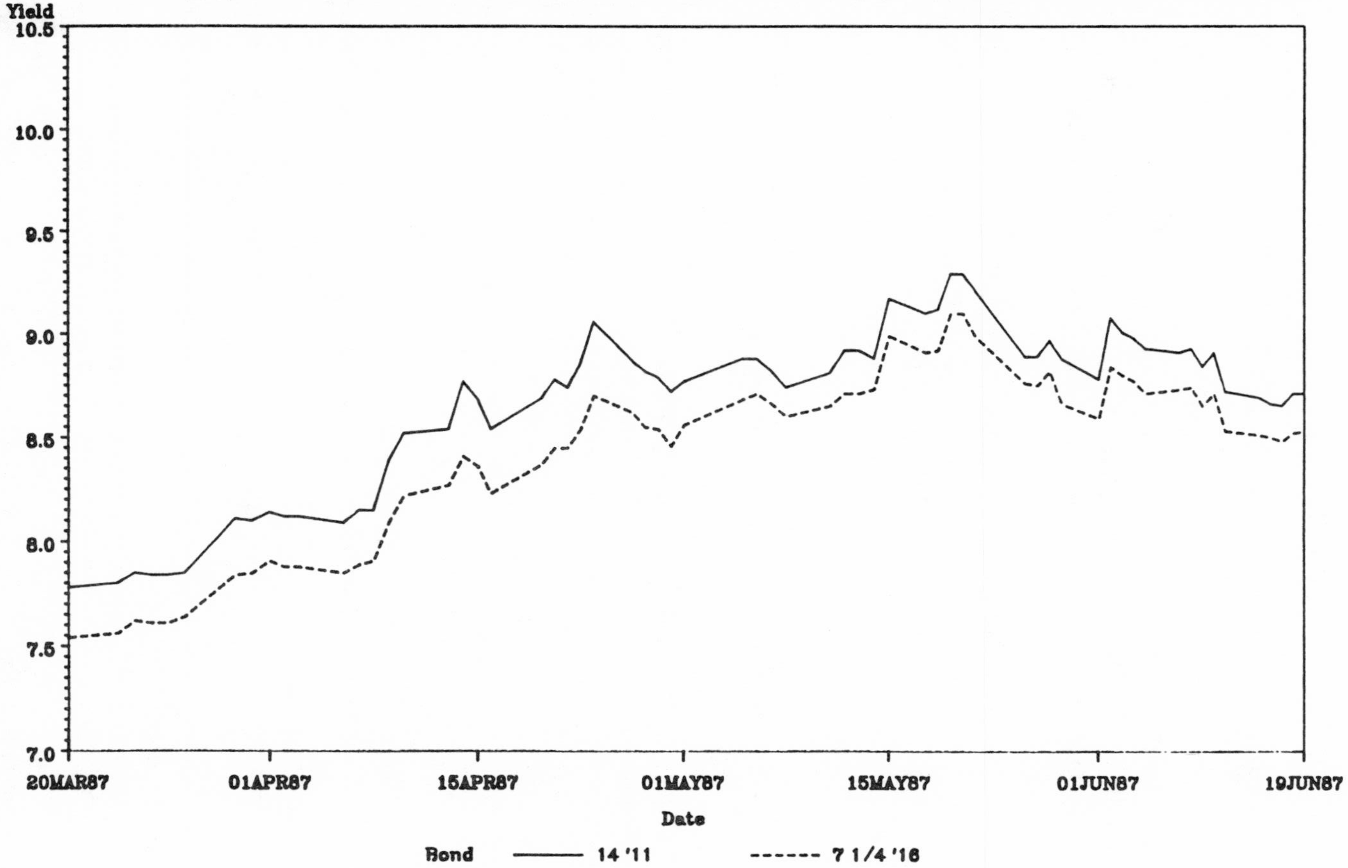

Bond ——— 14 '11   ----- 7 1/4 '16

September 1987 Cycle

Chart 6.3 shows that yields continued to rise on average through the third quarter, and on the last trading day of September, both the 7-1/4s and the 7-1/2s finished with a basis of 3/32nds, which made them the cheapest to deliver. All of the bonds delivered were the 7-1/4s. (See Table 6.3.)

The 12s of '13 finished with a basis of 76/32nds, and the 12-1/2s of '14 with a basis of 78/32nds. Those who were the short the basis with either of either the 12s or 12-1/2s (that is, the high-coupon, shorter maturity bonds) were caught by the shift in deliverables.

Table 6.3   September 1987 Bond Deliveries

DATE (YYMMDD)	COUPON	MATURITY	NUMBER DELIVERED	FACTOR
870930	7.25	5/15/16	4428	0.9163
870929	7.25	5/15/16	20	0.9163
870924	7.25	5/15/16	1	0.9163
870923	7.25	5/15/16	4	0.9163
Total Deliveries, Average Conversion Factor = 4453				0.9163

Source: Appendix I

December 1987 Cycle

The big story of the fourth quarter was the turmoil after the stock-market crash of October 19, which was followed by a rally in bonds. As yields fell, the bases of the 7-1/2s and 7-1/4s widened, while the basis of the 12s came in. (See Chart 6.4.)

Chart 6.3A   Basis for September 1987 Deliverable Bonds

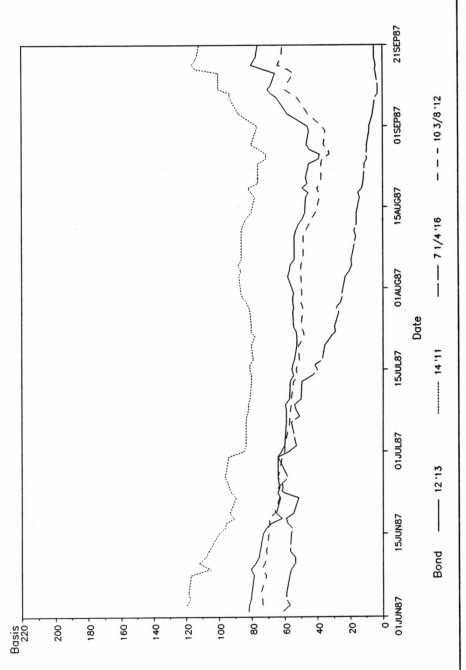

Basis

220
200
180
160
140
120
100
80
60
40
20
0

01JUN87   15JUN87   01JUL87   15JUL87   01AUG87   15AUG87   01SEP87   21SEP87

Date

Bond   ——— 12 '13   ········· 14 '11   ——— 7 1/4 '16   – – 10 3/8 '12

Chart 6.3B   Discount Corporation of New York Futures Yields for September 1987 Deliverable Bonds

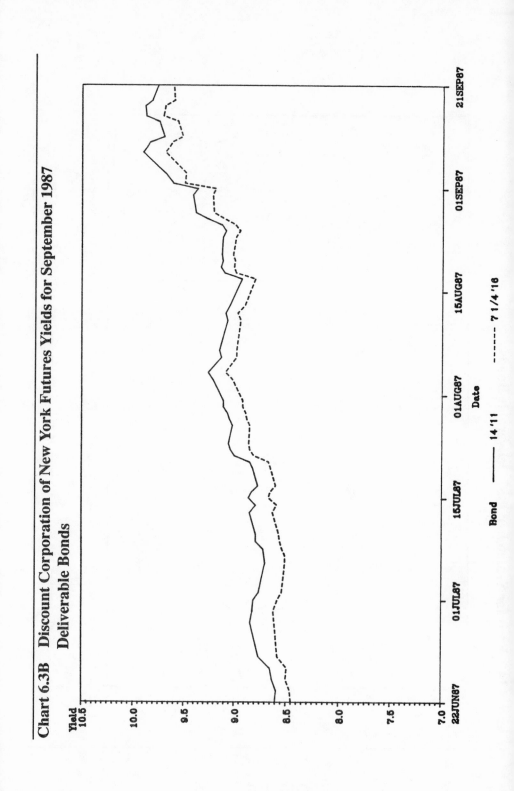

Yields went a little higher toward the end of the year, however, and
the quarter ended with the 7-1/4s as the cheapest to deliver on the last
trading day with a basis of 3/32nds. The 12s finished with a basis of
60/32nds. Table 6.4 shows that the 7-1/4s accounted for the bulk of
December deliveries.

Table 6.4   December 1987 Bond Deliveries

DATE (YYMMDD)	COUPON	MATURITY	NUMBER DELIVERED	FACTOR
871231	7.250	5/15/16	18119	0.9163
871230	7.250	5/15/16	2554	0.9163
871228	7.250	5/15/16	200	0.9163
871224	7.250	5/15/16	450	0.9163
871223	7.250	5/15/16	100	0.9163
871222	7.250	5/15/16	200	0.9163
871217	7.250	5/15/16	50	0.9163
871217	10.375	11/15/12-07	2	1.2336
871216	10.375	11/15/12-07	5500	1.2336
871216	7.250	5/15/16	1	0.9163
871214	10.375	11/15/12-07	256	1.2336
871211	10.375	11/15/12-07	250	1.2336
871209	7.250	5/15/16	90	0.9163
871208	7.250	5/15/16	4	0.9163
871207	7.250	5/15/16	49	0.9163
871204	7.250	5/15/16	50	0.9163
Total Deliveries, Average Conversion Factor =			27875	0.9847

Source: Appendix I

Chart 6.4A Basis for December 1987 Deliverable Bonds

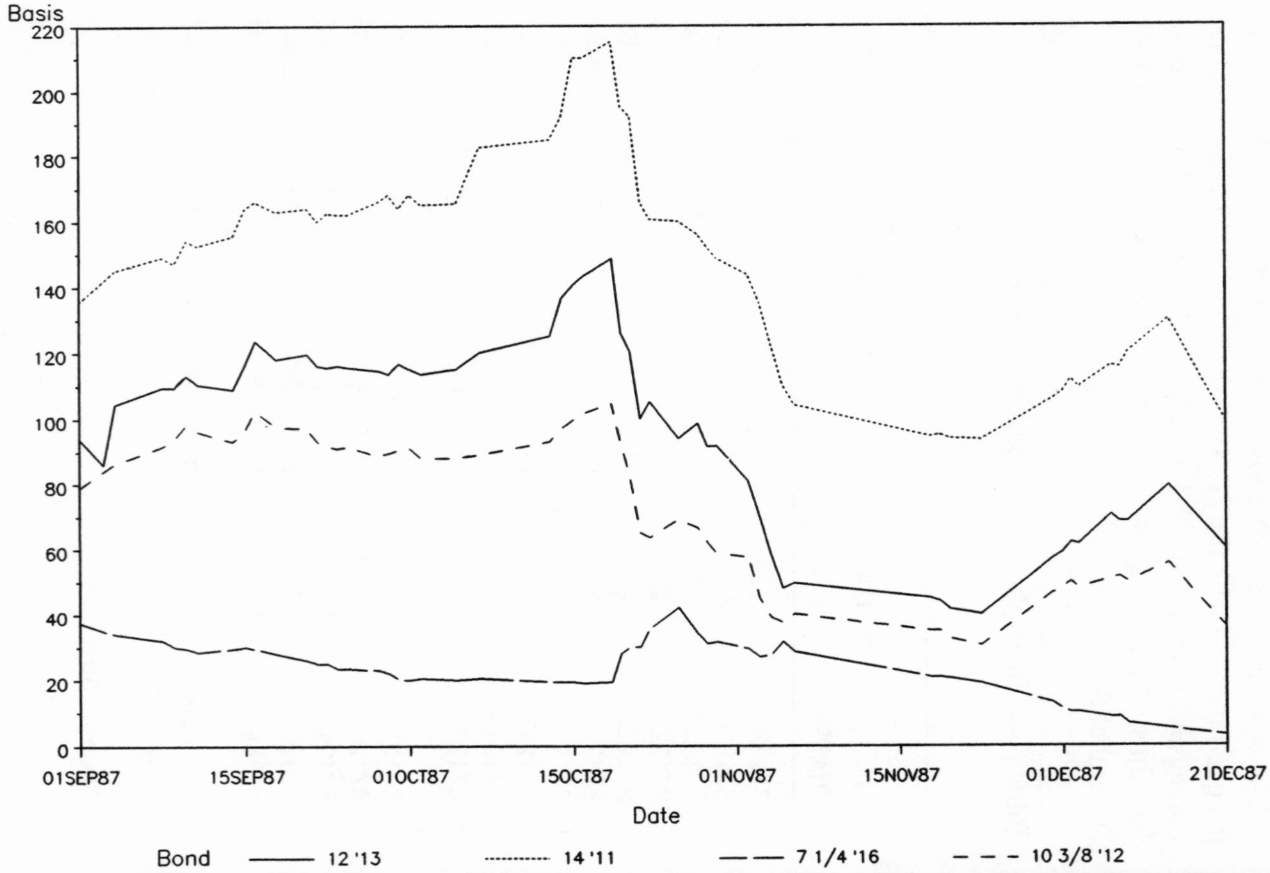

Basis

220
200
180
160
140
120
100
80
60
40
20
0

01SEP87   15SEP87   01OCT87   15OCT87   01NOV87   15NOV87   01DEC87   21DEC87

Date

Bond ——— 12'13   ········ 14'11   ——— 7 1/4'16   — — 10 3/8'12

Chart 6.4B Discount Corporation of New York Futures Yields for December 1987 Deliverable Bonds

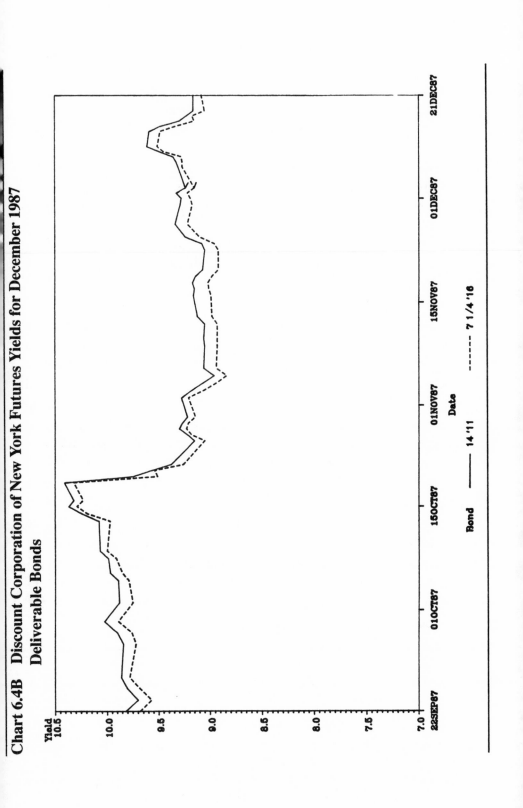

The basis of the 7-1/2s, which had been nearly indistinguishable from the 7-1/4s for much of the year, closed at 10/32nds on the last trading day (compared to 3/32nds for the 7-1/4s), reflecting a yield spread of about 2 basis points over the 7-1/4s. Two reasons generally are given for this differential: (1) most of the shorts who were caught by the widening bases of the 7-1/4s and the 7-1/2s were actually short the 7-1/2 basis and did not fully recover by the end of the year, and (2) the shorts' problems were compounded slightly by a minor short squeeze due to stripping of the 7-1/2s in October and November.

Mid-December Deliveries

The great delivery puzzle of December 1987 was the appearance early in the month of dribs and drabs of early deliveries followed by a huge block (5500) of the 10-3/8s of 11/12-07. The early deliveries were puzzling both because they were early in a positive carry setting and because some of the bonds—the 10-3/8s—were far from being cheap to deliver. The mid-month delivery of 10-3/8s into 5500 contracts, however, was astonishing. At the time, the basis of those bonds was just over 50/32nds, which is more than $1500 per contract that it cost the short to make delivery. On 5500 contracts, this amounted to more than $8 million.

The question on everyone's mind was Why? At this writing, the answer has not been nailed down, but the leading explanation both then and now is that the deliveries were made by a Japanese financial institution for accounting purposes. If so, the deliveries represent a stunning triumph of form over substance because the $8 million was real. The accounting picture was illusion.

Chapter 7

The Note Basis

The Chicago Board of Trade listed its 10-year Treasury Note contract for trading in 1982. The only difference between the note contract and the bond futures contracts is the definition of the deliverable grade. The Treasury note contract restricts delivery to original issue Treasury notes with at least 6-1/2 years but no more than 10 years remaining to maturity. Old Treasury bond issues with call or maturity dates that fall within this range are not eligible for delivery. In all other respects, the contract specifications are exactly the same as those for the bond contract. Conversion factors are used for calculating invoice prices, and the delivery schedule is the same.

As a result, any differences in the financial characteristics of the note and bond futures must be due to differences between deliverable notes and deliverable bonds. The differences that matter most stem from the fairly narrow range of deliverable maturities, from the no-call feature of all eligible Treasury notes, and from the naturally shorter maturities of the notes. The range of deliverable maturities is only 3-1/2 years, in contrast to the 15-year range for long-term Treasury bonds. Table 7.1 shows the notes that were eligible for delivery on February 19, 1988.

The practical effect of the narrower range is that the range of coupons on eligible notes tends to be quite a bit smaller than the range of coupons on eligible bonds. For the same reason, the range of conversion factors tends to be smaller for notes than for bonds. (See Table 7.2.)

Table 7.1 Deliverable Notes (February 19, 1988)

Delivery Month = March 1988
RP Rate = 6.650%

Trade Date = 2/19/88
Settlement Date = 2/22/88

First Delivery Date = 3/01/88 (Days Remaining = 8)
Futures Expiration Date = 3/22/88 (Days Remaining = 29)
Last Delivery Date = 3/30/88 (Days remaining = 38)

COUPON (1)	MATURITY (2)	CASH PRICE 2/19/88 (3)	CONVERSION FACTOR (4)	BASIS (5)	YIELD (6)	YIELD VALUE OF 32ND (7)	DOLLAR VALUE OF BASIS PT. (8)	DURATION (9)	CASH PRICE + ACCRUED INTEREST (10)	CARRY DOLLARS PER DAY (11)	CARRY 32nds PER DAY (12)	TOTAL CARRY 32nds/DAY TO LAST DELIVERY DAY (13)	IMPLIED RP RATE TO FIRST DELIVERY DAY (14)	IMPLIED RP RATE TO FUTURES EXPIRATION (15)	IMPLIED RP RATE TO LAST DELIVERY DAY (16)
						5-YEAR NOTE FUTURES (March Futures = 100 - 21/32nds or 42/64th)									
8.250	08/15/92	102.02	1.0090	18	7.696	0.00827	37.78	3.84	102.2212	37.82	0.121	4.599	-14.07	1.88	3.32
8.375	11/15/92	102.13	1.0142	10	7.745	0.00789	39.61	4.18	106.3454	33.64	0.108	4.090	-5.60	4.02	4.91
8.250	02/15/93	101.31	1.0099	10	7.750	0.00757	41.26	4.19	103.8312	34.85	0.112	4.238	-5.86	4.06	4.95
						10-YEAR NOTE FUTURES (March Futures = 97 - 23/32nds)									
9.500	10/15/94	107.08	1.0749	69	8.077	0.00590	52.95	4.98	110.5618	55.33	0.177	8.728	-79.01	-15.68	-9.94
11.625	11/15/94	118.10	1.1810	93	8.042	0.00547	57.08	4.89	121.4742	94.98	0.304	11.549	-98.24	-20.27	-13.23
8.625	01/15/95	103.01	1.0319	70	8.041	0.00588	53.16	5.32	103.9317	44.97	0.144	5.468	-86.87	-18.04	-11.63
11.250	02/15/95	118.22	1.1867	88	8.075	0.00538	58.07	5.17	116.9038	93.12	0.298	11.323	-93.63	-18.96	-12.22
11.250	05/15/95	116.30	1.1717	78	8.103	0.00524	59.68	5.18	119.9973	87.40	0.280	10.628	-82.28	-18.00	-10.02
10.500	08/15/95	112.31	1.1353	65	8.150	0.00523	59.72	5.49	113.1707	79.41	0.254	9.656	-71.51	-13.10	-7.83
9.500	11/15/95	107.14	1.0834	50	8.179	0.00528	59.15	5.60	110.0213	57.76	0.185	7.023	-55.68	-9.19	-4.99
8.875	02/15/96	103.29	1.0496	43	8.198	0.00528	59.18	5.92	104.0789	51.57	0.165	6.270	-49.56	-7.56	-3.79
7.375	05/15/96	94.28	0.9636	23	8.242	0.00548	57.01	6.13	96.8608	23.65	0.078	2.876	-25.62	-1.83	0.53
7.250	11/15/96	93.22	0.9544	14	8.277	0.00531	58.63	6.40	95.6593	22.47	0.072	2.733	-12.51	1.96	3.27
8.500	05/15/97	101.05	1.0316	11	8.315	0.00488	64.07	6.45	103.4681	42.39	0.136	5.154	-7.10	3.91	4.90
8.625	08/15/97	102.01	1.0401	13	8.311	0.00476	65.59	6.68	102.1971	48.17	0.154	5.857	-9.02	3.54	4.67
8.875	11/15/97	103.23	1.0575	12	8.307	0.00463	67.48	6.62	106.1326	47.77	0.153	5.809	-7.91	3.79	4.85
8.125	02/15/98	99.04	1.0082	19	8.255	0.00468	66.73	7.00	99.2813	39.82	0.127	4.842	-19.35	0.51	2.30

NOTE : 2.00 PM (CST) CASH PRICES ARE MARKED BETWEEN THE BID AND OFFER
YIELDS ARE CALCULATED TO MATURITY FOR DISCOUNT SECURITIES AND TO THE CALL DATE FOR PREMIUM SECURITIES.
COST OF CARRY IS PER $ 1 MILLION FACE VALUE, AND IS SHOWN AS $/DAY, 32nd/DAY AND TOTAL 32nd/DAY AND TOTAL DELIVERY DATE IN 32nds.
COURTESY OF DCNYF RESEARCH GROUP.

Table 7.2 Conversion Factors for Deliverable Notes for Various Contracts Months

COUPON	MATURITY	MAR'88	JUN'88	SEP'88	DEC'88	MAR'89	JUN'89	SEP'89	DEC'89
9-1/2%	10/15/94	1.0749							
11-5/8%	11/15/94	1.1810							
8-5/8%	01/15/95	1.0319	1.0312						
11-1/4%	02/15/95	1.1667	1.1623						
11-1/4%	05/15/95	1.1717	1.1667	1.1623					
10-1/2%	08/15/95	1.1353	1.1320	1.1282	1.1248				
9-1/2%	11/15/95	1.0834	1.0811	1.0792	1.0768	1.0749			
8-7/8%	02/15/96	1.0496	1.0486	1.0472	1.0462	1.0447	1.0437		
7-3/8%	05/15/96	.9636	.9642	.9653	.9659	.9670	.9677	.9688	
7-1/4%	11/15/96	.9544	.9552	.9563	.9571	.9583	.9592	.9604	.9613
8-1/2%	05/15/97	1.0316	1.0308	1.0304	1.0296	1.0291	1.0283	1.0278	1.0269
8-5/8%	08/15/97	1.0401	1.0396	1.0386	1.0380	1.0370	1.0364	1.0354	1.0347
8-7/8%	11/15/97	1.0575	1.0562	1.0554	1.0541	1.0532	1.0519	1.0510	1.0496
8-1/8%	02/15/98	1.0082	1.0082	1.0079	1.0079	1.0076	1.0076	1.0072	1.0073

All eligible notes were issued with complete call protection. That is, the Treasury cannot redeem any of the notes before maturity. The effect of the no-call feature of Treasury notes is a less volatile swing in duration as the notes change from premium to discount securities as their prices pass through par.

The shorter maturity of the notes translates directly into lower durations for notes than for bonds. For the same level of yield volatility, note prices will be less volatile than bond prices. For the purposes of studying the note basis, the shorter maturities of the notes also imply conversion factors that are closer to 1.000. For example, a note with a 12-percent coupon will trade closer to par than a bond with a 12-percent coupon.

Taken together, these differences between notes and bonds account for the following differences between note and bond futures:

- Note futures prices are less volatile than bond futures. Equal changes in yields produce much smaller price swings in note futures than in bond futures. Futures price limits in note futures are seldom if ever hit.

- The note basis is more predictable.

- The short's options are worth far less in note futures than in bond futures, in part because note prices are less volatile and in part because their conversion factors tend to be closer to 1.000 and clustered closer together than are bond conversion factors.

With one possible exception, the wild card has never been played in notes. The shifting deliverables effect is present but worth less because the price changes produced by swings in yields are smaller. The switch option is similarly worth less.

Table 7.3, which is for notes what Table 2.2 is for bonds, illustrates the predictability of the note basis. Those tables show what happens to the cheapest to deliver note at the expiration of futures trading as yields rise and fall. The only difference between the two tables is that Table

Table 7.3 Assessing Shifts in the Cheapest to Deliver Note (2/19/88)

ISSUE		CURRENT MARKET (2/19/88)			BASIS PROJECTIONS FOR A CHANGE IN YIELDS (In Basis Points)													
					-200		-100		-50		0		+50		+100		+200	
COUPON	MATURITY	PRICE	YIELD	BASIS	YIELD	BASIS	YIELD	BASIS	YIELD	BASIS	YIELD	BASIS	YIELD	BASIS	YIELD	BASIS	YIELD	BASIS
9.500	10/15/94	107.06	8.077	69	6.077	2	7.077	9	7.577	34	8.077	58	8.577	81	9.077	104	10.077	149
11.625	11/15/94	118.10	8.042	93	6.042	9	7.042	21	7.542	50	8.042	77	8.542	105	9.042	132	10.042	184
8.625	01/15/95	103.01	8.041	70	6.041	24	7.041	22	7.541	42	8.041	60	8.541	79	9.041	97	10.041	134
11.250	02/15/95	116.22	8.075	86	6.075	15	7.075	20	7.575	46	8.075	70	8.575	95	9.075	119	10.075	166
11.250	05/15/95	116.30	8.103	78	6.103	18	7.103	18	7.603	42	8.103	63	8.603	86	9.103	108	10.103	152
10.500	05/15/95	112.31	8.150	65	6.150	21	7.150	14	7.650	33	8.150	51	8.650	71	9.150	89	10.150	126
9.500	08/15/95	107.14	8.179	50	6.179	26	7.179	11	7.679	25	8.179	39	8.679	54	9.179	68	10.179	99
8.875	11/15/95	103.29	8.198	43	6.198	34	7.198	11	7.698	22	8.198	32	8.698	44	9.198	55	10.198	80
7.375	02/15/96	94.28	8.242	23	6.242	37	7.242	5	7.742	11	8.242	16	8.742	22	9.242	28	10.242	44
7.250	05/15/96	93.22	8.277	14	6.277	46	7.277	5	7.777	6	8.277	7	8.777	9	9.277	12	10.277	22
8.500	05/15/97	101.05	8.315	11	6.315	49	7.315	2	7.815	2	8.315	2	8.815	4	9.315	7	10.315	16
8.625	08/15/97	102.01	8.311	13	6.311	58	7.311	6	7.811	4	8.311	3	8.811	4	9.311	5	10.311	12
8.875	11/15/97	103.23	8.307	12	6.307	65	7.307	9	7.807	5	8.307	2	8.807	2	9.307	2	10.307	8
8.125	02/15/98	99.04	8.255	19	6.255	88	7.255	25	7.755	17	8.255	10	8.755	6	9.255	3	10.255	2

Note Futures Price 97.23 | 109.32 | 104.14 | 101.05 | 97.32 | 94.29 | 91.29 | 86.05

*This report is available daily from DCNYF.
Source DCNYF Research

7.3 assumes that the basis of the cheapest to deliver note at final settlement is 2/32nds (instead of the 6/32nds that Table 2.2 assumed for
bonds).

Given market conditions on February 19, two issues would be equally cheap to deliver at the expiration of futures trading: the 8-1/2s of
5/97 and the 8-7/8s of 11/97. The 8-5/8s of 8/97 would be a very close
second. What Table 7.3 shows, however, is that the bases of these notes
are comparatively insensitive to changes in the level of yields. For example, a 100-basis-point rise in yields leaves the 8-7/8s cheapest to
deliver while increasing the basis of the 8-1/2s to 7/32nds. A 100-basis-
point drop in yields leaves the 8-1/2s cheapest to deliver while increasing the basis of the 8-7/8s to only 9/32nds. When compared with the
potential swings in bond bases as yields rise or fall, these ranges are
really quite small.

The comparative stability of note futures and the low value of the
short's options are clearly reflected in the generally higher implied repo
rates for cheapest to deliver notes. Table 7.4 shows the implied repo
rates for the five cheapest to deliver notes and the five cheapest to
deliver bonds. Table 7.4 reveals two things: (1) the highest implied repo
rate for the cheapest to deliver note was 4.90% compared to 3.96% for
the cheapest to deliver bond, and (2) the implied repo rates for the next
cheapest notes fall off much less quickly than the implied repo rates
for the bonds.

Relative Importance of Anticipated New Issues

One area in which note futures have distinguished themselves from
bond futures is in the importance of the anticipated new issue. As Chapter 3 notes, the emergence of a new bond issue typically takes place in
a yield setting that works against its being the cheapest to deliver. High
yields favor the delivery of long-duration bonds, and the long maturity
of a new issue clearly works in this direction. At the same time, the
high coupon on a new bond issued in a high-yield market tends to

Table 7.4   Implied Repo Rates for 5 Cheapest to Deliver Issues (2/19/88)

RANK	BONDS		NOTES	
	ISSUE	IMPLIED REPO RATE	ISSUE	IMPLIED REPO RATE
1	10-3/8 of 11/12-07	3.96	8-1/2 of 5/97	4.90
2	12 of 8/13-08	1.79	8-7/8 of 11/97	4.85
3	11-3/4 of 11/14-09	1.41	8-5/8 of 8/97	4.67
4	10-3/8 of 11/09-04	.91	7-1/4 of 11/96	3.27
5	13-1/4 of 5/14-09	.76	8-1/8 of 2/98	2.30

reduce its duration. The wide range of coupons on deliverable issues usually means that a somewhat older issue but with a substantially lower coupon will be the cheapest to deliver when yields are high.

For much of 1984 and the first half of 1985, the combination of high but falling interest rates worked together to make the "new guy" the cheapest to deliver for five consecutive deliver months. (See Table 7.5 in which the most recently issued note was also the most heavily delivered note.) High interest rates naturally favored the deliver of long-duration notes. Falling interest rates meant that the newest note had not only the longest maturity but also, because of the narrow range of deliverable maturities, the lowest coupon. Together, the high duration and relatively low coupon worked to make the newest note the cheapest to deliver.

In a high but falling interest-rate setting, then, the characteristics of the anticipated new issue would be a major driving force in determining the futures price. Similarly, although the events have not come together at the same time, low but rising interest rates could work together to make the new issue cheapest to deliver.

Unusual Expiration of September 1986

Perhaps the single most unusual event in the life of Treasury note futures took place during the last three minutes of trading of the September 1986 futures contract. The result was possibly the only opportunity to play the wild card in note futures. It was not, however, a conventional wild card.

In a conventional wild card play, the opportunity is created by the cash market making a substantial move after the futures price is fixed for the day. In the case of September 1986 note futures, a wild card opportunity was created by a substantial last-minute rise in the futures price that was accompanied by no change in the cash market.

Table 7.5

DELIVERY MONTH	MOST HEAVILY DELIVERED NOTE
Mar '83	13-3/4 of 5/92
Jun '83	10-1/8 of 5/93
Sep '83	11-7/8 of 8/93 *
Dec '83	11-3/4 of 11/93
Mar '84	11-3/4 of 11/93
Jun '84	13-1/8 of 5/94 *
Sep '84	12-5/8 of 8/94 *
Dec '84	11-5/8 of 11/94 *
Mar '85	11-1/4 of 2/95 *
Jun '85	11-1/4 of 5/95 *
Sep '85	11-1/4 of 5/95
Dec '85	10-1/2 of 8/95
Mar '86	13-1/8 of 5/94
Jun '86	11-3/4 of 11/93
Sep '86	12-5/8 of 8/94
Dec '86	13-1/8 of 5/94
Mar '87	11-3/4 of 11/93
Jun '87	7-1/4 of 11/96
Sep '87	7-1/4 of 11/96
Dec '87	7-1/4 of 11/96
Mar '88	8-7/8 of 11/97

* Indicates newest Issue

Setting

In an otherwise quiet market on Friday, September 19, 1986, the settlement price of the note contract was bid during the last three minutes of trading from a price of 100-27/32nds to 101-25/32nds. The final settlement price was set at 101-10/32nds. Thus, the settlement price was forced up almost half a point, with the bidding of two major institutional players responsible for the increase.

At the time, there was much confusion about who would gain from such a move, who would lose, and how much.

Paradoxically, even though the settlement price is higher, it is not the person who is still long at the expiration of trading in the September futures contract who benefits from the price increase. In this instance, the price action made the longs roughly $1 million worse off and the shorts $1 million better off.

Long Loss from Price Increase

To understand why the longs were made worse off, it is important to know two things. First, the underlying cash market did not move during the settlement gyration. Second, any open longs were required to take delivery of notes at the closing settlement price.

How much did it matter? In September 1986, the most likely note to be delivered had a conversion factor of 1.263. The effect of the increase in the futures price of 15/32nds was to increase in the invoice price of the deliverable note by 19/32nds. That is, the longs had to pay 19/32nds more than they would have had to without the last-minute price increase. On 10,000 contracts, this would amount to an extra invoice amount of $5,920,312.50. Only part of this, however, was released back to the long the next morning in the form of variation margin payments. The 15/32nds increase in the futures price would bring in $4,687,500 to the holders of 10,000 long note futures position. The net incremented bill that the long ended up paying would therefore be

$1,232,812.50 to obtain securities whose cash market value had not changed!

As it turned out, deliveries were made on 9,234 contracts including these:

- 4,902 of the 12-5/8ths of 8/94
- 2,442 of the 13-1/8ths of 5/94
- 1,740 of the 11-3/4s of 11/93

together with 140 of the 11-1/4s of 5/95 and 10 of the 11-1/4s of 2/95. All three of the most heavily-delivered notes had conversion factors substantially greater than 1. As a result, the loss to the longs all of which accrues to the shorts was about $1 million.

The lesson of all this is that settlements must be closely watched on all contracts (not just the stock-index futures, which were settling on the same day and which got all of the attention while this play was going on). Whatever the motives of the late buyers of note futures contracts, the effect of their actions was to enrich the shorts (including possibly themselves) at the expense of the longs.

Chapter 8

Applications for Portfolio Managers

An initial observation of this book was that primary government securities dealers have been short the bond basis since 1985 and that by the end of 1987 the size of their short position had reached approximately $8 billion. With implied repo rates on the cheapest to deliver running about three percentage points below the general collateral repo rate, the gross income from being short $8 billion of the basis is $240 million a year.

This is not, of course, free money. Being short the basis means taking long futures positions. Because all implicit timing and delivery options belong to whoever is short the futures contract (see Chapters 2 and 3), the trader who sells the basis is, in effect, selling those options. Whenever any one of the timing or delivery options finishes in the money, the result is a reduction in the profitability of being short the basis. If the options finish deep enough in the money, a short basis position can produce a loss.

The large short basis position that the dealers have maintained over the past few years, however, suggests that selling the options has on balance been a profitable thing to do.

Lessons for Portfolio Managers

Yield Enhancement   This chapter shows how the lessons learned by the dealers can be applied to bond portfolio management. We focus on yield enhancement, which is nothing more than replacing a long bond position with a position in long futures and short-term money market investments. One way to look at this trade is that the portfolio manager is using the proceeds of selling the bonds to finance other people's holdings of those bonds. The portfolio manager is getting out of the bond business, however. If the hedge ratios are calculated correctly, the duration of the long futures position is the same as the duration of the cash bond portfolio that it replaces.

From the perspective of this book, a yield enhancement trade is equivalent to selling the basis, which is what the government securities dealers have done, with the exception that the bonds are sold out of portfolio rather than sold short. The risk/return characteristics of a yield enhancement strategy are the same as those of shorting the basis, but the consequences of being wrong can be substantially less dire.

Hedging   The profitability of the yield enhancement strategy also has clear implications for both anticipatory and short hedging. To the extent the futures price is too low, a portfolio manager who uses futures to go long the bond market in anticipation of receiving funds to manage will earn a premium over what could have been earned in the bond market. For the same reason, a portfolio manager who uses futures to hedge a long bond position will give up more yield than would be lost by selling the bonds out of portfolio and investing the proceeds in the RP market.

How Yield Enhancement Works

Anyone who is naturally long bonds, unless constrained by charters or regulation, has two choices:

- Hold the bonds.
- Sell the bonds, go long futures, invest the proceeds short term, and buy back the bonds at a later date.

In both cases, the bond holder starts with the bonds and ends with exactly the same bonds. The second approach, if it provides the investor with more money at the end, is said to enhance the yield on the bond. Yield enhancement, then, is a strategy in which a natural long position in bonds is replaced with an appropriate long position in futures together with an investment in short-term money market instruments.

The driving force behind yield enhancement is the premium in the basis. Chart 8.1 illustrates the typical relationship—for a positive yield curve setting—between the current spot price of the cheapest to deliver, carry to expiration of the futures contract, and the market futures price. For this illustration, assume that the bond carries an 8 percent coupon and has a conversion factor of 1.000.

The bond's basis is the distance between A and C. Carry to expiration, however, is only the distance between A and B. The rest of the basis, or the premium, is the distance between B and C. From a strict carry standpoint, the futures price is too low. One could sell the bond at A, finance the short position at a cost of A − B, and buy the futures contract at C. At expiration, when the spot and futures prices come together, and if there has been no change in the cheapest to deliver, the short basis trader will make B − C. The short basis trader will make the premium.

Yield Enhancement with Cheapest to Deliver

This and other examples show how the trade works for $100,000 face value of the bond and assume that the trader can do fractions of futures. This isn't possible, of course, but basis trades done for yield enhancement would involve substantially larger amounts of money so that the number of futures bought can be quite close to the bond's conversion factor.

The first step in yield enhancement with the cheapest to deliver is to sell the cash bond and take a long futures position equal to the bond's conversion factor for each $100,000 par value of the bonds sold. In this case, the cheapest to deliver bond was the 7-1/4s of '16, which had a price including accrued interest of 82.0893 on December 23, 1987. The

Chart 8.1   Basis, Carry, and Premium of Cheapest to Deliver (8% Coupon Bond)

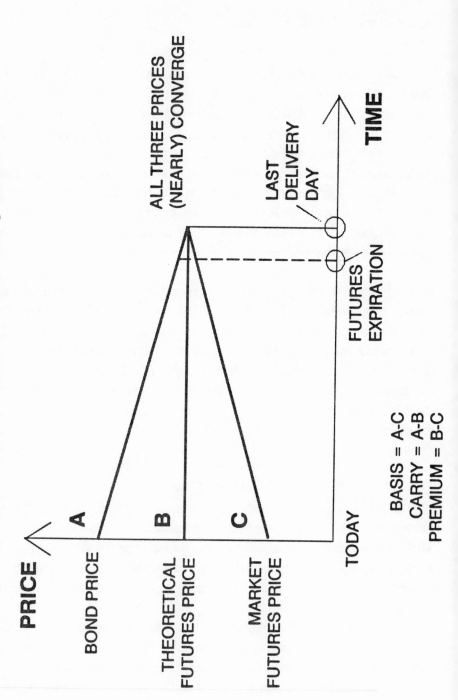

PRICE

A — BOND PRICE

B — THEORETICAL FUTURES PRICE

C — MARKET FUTURES PRICE

ALL THREE PRICES (NEARLY) CONVERGE

LAST DELIVERY DAY

FUTURES EXPIRATION

TODAY

TIME

BASIS = A-C
CARRY = A-B
PREMIUM = B-C

bond's conversion factor was 0.9167, and the March futures price was 87-18/32nds.

At these prices, the basis of the cheapest to deliver was 33/32nds. Given a repo rate of 7 percent, total carry to last delivery day was 12.279/32nds. The premium in the bond, then, was 20.721/32nds.

What would the total return have been from December 23, 1987, to March 21, 1988 on the yield enhancement trade? The proceeds from selling the 7-1/4s in December were $82,089. At an *average* repo rate over the holding period of 6.7 percent, the total amount earned would have been $1,375. On March 21, principal plus interest would have been $83,464[=$82,089 + $1,375]. Add to this the amount made or lost on the futures. Futures increased from 87-18/32nds to 91-25/32nds so that the gain on 0.9167 contracts would have been $3,867.

Altogether, the yield enhancing trade would have produced total cash from all sources equal to $87,331, a total increase of $5,242, for a quarterly return of 6.4 percent.

Compare this with what the long bond would have provided over the same period. The total price of the 7-1/4s on March 21—price plus accrued interest—amounted to $86,913.

Thus, holding on to the bond would have produced total cash equal to $86,913, a total increase of $4,824, for a quarterly return of 5.9 percent.

The portfolio manager could have bought the bonds back in for $86,913 and had an additional $418 left over for each $100,000 face value of the 7-1/4s used in the yield enhancement trade.

The comparison can also be expressed in annual rates of return. In this case, the rate of return to simply holding the bond over the three months from December to March was 25.8 percent. The rate of return to the yield enhancement trade was 28.2 percent.

Yield enhancement added 2.4 annual percentage points to the total return on the 7-1/4s of '16.

Yield Enhancement with a Non-Cheap Bond

The main difference between yield enhancement with non-cheap bonds is in the number of futures to go long. Rather than using the non-cheap bond's conversion factor, this example uses a hedge ratio calculated based on the yield values of a 32nd for the non-cheap and cheapest to deliver bonds and the conversion factor of the cheapest to deliver. (See Chapter 4.) Apart from this, the transactions are the same.

Consider a yield enhancement trading involving the 14s of 11/11-06. The conversion factor of these bonds was 1.5743. The appropriate hedge ratio on December 23, 1987, however, was 1.281. Hedge ratios must be monitored and adjusted to compensate for changes in the level of yields and for any changes in the cheapest to deliver. In this case, by the time the trade was unwound on March 21, 1988, the appropriate hedge ratio had fallen to 1.247. As a result, a yield enhancement trade with the 14s would have required selling $100,000 face value of the bonds out of portfolio, investing the proceeds in the RP market, and going long 1.281 futures. Assuming that the average futures position over the period was 1.264 contracts and that the proceeds of the bond sale were invested at an average RP rate of 6.7 percent, the transactions would have added $407, or 134 annualized basis points to the total return to holding $100,000 par value of the 14s.

In this particular example, bond and futures prices rose. Those inclined to second-guess trades might complain that the trade would have been more profitable had the bond's conversion factor rather than its hedge ratio been used in constructing the trade. The response to such a complaint, of course, is that prices might just as well have fallen. The reason for using the hedge ratio rather than the conversion factor for a non-cheap bond is to put in place a trade that performs as expected whether prices rise or fall. We want a trade that works whether yields rise, fall, or stay the same.

Yield Enhancement with a Portfolio

Although yield enhancement can work with a single bond, an approach that is likely to prove more prudent is to undertake yield enhancement with a portfolio of bonds. Diversification will require giving up the big winners, but the reward is protection against serious losses in the event of a short squeeze or unexpected widening of yield spreads for any other reason.

Tables 8.1, 8.2, and 8.3 show the results of yield enhancement for three different sets of circumstances. The first is the first quarter of 1988, when yields were generally falling. The second is the second quarter, when yields were generally rising. The third is the second quarter of 1986, during which the infamous short squeeze of the 9-1/4s of '16 was in full swing.

Each case assumes that six different bonds have been sold out of the portfolio, the proceeds invested in the reverse RP market, and the long positions replaced by futures. These illustrations involve bonds with a range of coupons, maturities, and call protection. For the cheapest to deliver, the number of futures was reckoned as the bond's conversion factor. For all non-cheap bonds, the number of futures was reckoned as the bond's hedge ratio, which was calculated using yield values of a 32nd together with the conversion factor of the cheapest to deliver.

During the first quarter of 1988, yield enhancement added anywhere from 131 to 350 annualized basis points to the yields of the various bonds in the portfolio. (See Table 8.1.) The raw total return averaged 23.82 percent for the bonds themselves. The average enhanced return was 26.34 percent. Altogether, then, yield enhancement added 2.52 percent to the annualized total return to the portfolio.

The exercise also works when yields are rising and bond prices are falling. (See Table 8.2.) From March 1988 through May 1988, the average raw return to the same six bonds was –25.33 percent. The enhanced return, in contrast, was –23.55 percent. In other words, the enhanced return was 178 annualized basis points greater than the raw portfolio return.

Table 8.1 Yield Enhancement with a Portfolio/Falling Yields (12/23/87 to 3/21/88)

ISSUE	RAW RETURN	ENHANCED RETURN (annualized)	DIFFERENCE
14s of 11/11-06	22.00	23.31	1.31
10-3/8s of 11/12-07	22.32	24.67	2.35
10-5/8s of 8/15	22.79	26.29	3.50
7-1/4s of 5/16	25.66	28.10	2.44
7-1/2s of 11/16	25.32	28.40	3.08
8-7/8s of 8/17	24.82	27.28	2.46
AVERAGE	23.82	26.34	2.52

Table 8.2 Yield Enhancement with a Portfolio/Rising Yields (2/29/88 to 5/27/88)

ISSUE	RAW RETURN	ENHANCED RETURN (annualized)	DIFFERENCE
14s of 11/11-06	-21.22	-19.45	1.77
10-3/8s of 11/12-07	-22.26	-20.82	1.44
10-5/8s of 8/15	-25.98	-23.96	2.02
7-1/4s of 5/16	-27.35	-25.43	1.92
7-1/2s of 11/16	-27.45	-25.82	1.63
8-7/8s of 8/17	-27.72	-25.80	1.92
AVERAGE	-25.33	-23.55	1.78

The acid test for yield enhancement may well have been experienced during the spring of 1986 when the short squeeze of the 9-1/4s of 2/16 was in full swing. Yields were generally falling, but a comparatively tight grip by Japanese institutions on the 9-1/4s cause their yields to fall by more than the yields on comparable bonds. As a result, the raw return on the 9-1/4s was 17.83 percent from March 19 through June 19, while the enhanced return was only 8.35 percent. The portfolio manager would have given up the opportunity to earn 948 annualized basis points of return on the 9-1/4s by selling them out of portfolio and replacing them with futures.

The loss was largely, although not entirely, offset by diversification, however. For the sample six-bond portfolio, the overall loss was 115 annualized basis points. (See Table 8.3.) Yield enhancement still added 236 basis points to the yield of the 14s and 170 basis points to the yield of the 13-1/4s. Thus, even with the awful performance of the 9-1/4s, and the dismal performance of the 10-5/8s, the enhanced portfolio fell only slightly behind the raw portfolio.

To put these results into perspective, remember that the short squeeze of the 9-1/4s ranks as perhaps the bloodiest disaster in the recorded history of basis trading. During that episode, a basis trader who was outright short the 9-1/4s against long futures actually lost almost 2.5 percent of the price of the bond.

For a portfolio manager, however, the picture looked less gloomy. For one thing, diversification would have softened the effect of the squeeze. For another, the portfolio manager was not compelled to replace the 9-1/4s. Instead, the 9-1/4s could have been replaced with a bond of similar coupon and maturity. The chief effect of having sold out the bonds would have been the lost opportunity to hold the 9-1/4s and swap out of them when their spread widened so dramatically against the yields of other bonds.

The squeeze was transitory. Had the 9-1/4s not been swapped out of portfolio, the raw return on these bonds in the next quarter was decided lower than the raw returns on other bonds. Much of the loss in return

Table 8.3   Yield Enhancement with a Portfolio/Short Squeeze of '86 (3/19/86 to 6/19/86)

ISSUE	RAW RETURN	ENHANCED RETURN (annualized)	DIFFERENCE
9-1/4s of 2/16	17.83	8.35	-9.48
12-1/2s of 8/14-09	7.76	8.19	.43
14s of 11/11-06	5.75	8.11	2.36
10-3/8s of 11/12-07	7.63	8.18	.55
13-1/4s of 5/14-09	6.46	8.16	1.70
10-5/8s of 8/15	9.42	8.29	-1.13
AVERAGE	9.37	8.22	-1.15

would have been made up during the next quarter when yield spreads came back into line.

On balance, then, the expected income from yield enhancement strategies appears to have been substantial while the risks associated with the timing and delivery options have been slight.

Caveats

A few words of caution are in order.

First, gains and losses on a long bond position are unrealized as long as the portfolio manager holds the bonds. Gains and losses on a long futures position are marked to market daily. That is, gains produce cash inflows that must be invested short term while losses require cash to paid out. As a result, yield enhancement entails active cash management while a straight, long bond portfolio does not.

Second, the size of the bond futures market is large but not unlimited. At this writing, open interest in the bond futures contract—the total number of contracts open—was just over 400,000. At $100,000 face value bonds per contract, open interest in the bond futures contract amounts to roughly $40 billion worth of Treasury bonds. A large increase in the demand for bond futures by portfolio managers pursuing yield enhancement strategies would almost certainly bid up the futures price relative to the prices of the actual bonds. A sufficiently large increase in the demand for long bond futures would, of course, reduce the profitability of yield enhancement strategies to zero and could tip the balance the other way.

Third, gains and losses on futures are treated differently for tax purposes than gains and losses on actual bonds. Whether the incremental yield from pursuing yield enhancement strategies really represents an increase in after-tax yields depends on the tax status of the institution.

Even so, in a market where the distance between the best and worst portfolio managers is often measured in tens of annualized basis points, the prospect of adding 100 to 200 basis points to the yield of a Treasury bond portfolio merits attention.

Hedging

If a portfolio manager can consistently make money by replacing physical Treasury bonds with long futures positions, then hedgers who use futures will consistently make or lose money depending on how they use the market.

Anticipatory Hedging

Buying futures in anticipation of taking a long position in the underlying commodity is a standard practice for many portfolio managers. The alternative to buying Treasury bond futures is a leveraged purchase of the bonds themselves. The lesson from the preceding discussion of yield enhancement is that buying the futures has been more profitable on average than buying the bonds. As long as yield enhancement is profitable, any long bond futures position is likely to be preferable to a long position in the bonds themselves.

Short Hedging

The classic example of hedging is to sell futures against a natural long position in the underlying. If the yield enhancement strategy described in this chapter is profitable, however, selling bond futures is not a good long-term alternative to selling the bonds themselves.

Bond futures can still provide good short-term hedges, of course. The market is extremely liquid. Moreover, a portfolio manager can avoid recognizing gains or losses on individual bonds by selling futures rather than selling bonds out of portfolio.

Appendix I
History of CBOT Bond Deliveries
December 1977—June 1988

DISCOUNT CORPORATION OF NEW YORK FUTURES

History of CBOT Bond Deliveries, December 1977 To June 1988

---------------------------------- Delivery Quarter=1988Q2 ----------------------------------

OBS	Date	Coupon	Maturity	Number Delivered	Factor
1	880630	7.25	5/15/16	21005	0.9167
2	880628	7.25	5/15/16	1	0.9167
Total Deliveries, Average Conversion Factor =				21006	0.9167

---------------------------------- Delivery Quarter=1988Q1 ----------------------------------

OBS	Date	Coupon	Maturity	Number Delivered	Factor
3	880331	10.375	11/15/12-07	7137	1.2326
4	880331	7.250	5/15/16	50	0.9167
5	880330	10.375	11/15/12-07	110	1.2326
6	880330	7.250	5/15/16	1	0.9167
7	880329	7.250	5/15/16	200	0.9167
8	880328	7.250	5/15/16	2	0.9167
9	880318	12.000	8/15/13-08	100	1.3976
10	880318	7.250	5/15/16	50	0.9167
11	880318	10.375	11/15/12-07	50	1.2326
12	880309	7.250	5/15/16	10	0.9167
13	880301	13.250	5/15/14-09	3	1.5299
Total Deliveries, Average Conversion Factor =				7713	1.2220

---------------------------------- Delivery Quarter=1987Q4 ----------------------------------

OBS	Date	Coupon	Maturity	Number Delivered	Factor
14	871231	7.250	5/15/16	18119	0.9163
15	871230	7.250	5/15/16	2554	0.9163
16	871228	7.250	5/15/16	200	0.9163
17	871224	7.250	5/15/16	450	0.9163
18	871223	7.250	5/15/16	100	0.9163
19	871222	7.250	5/15/16	200	0.9163
20	871217	7.250	5/15/16	50	0.9163
21	871217	10.375	11/15/12-07	2	1.2336
22	871216	10.375	11/15/12-07	5500	1.2336
23	871216	7.250	5/15/16	1	0.9163
24	871214	10.375	11/15/12-07	256	1.2336
25	871211	10.375	11/15/12-07	250	1.2336
26	871209	7.250	5/15/16	90	0.9163
27	871208	7.250	5/15/16	4	0.9163
28	871207	7.250	5/15/16	49	0.9163
29	871204	7.250	5/15/16	50	0.9163
Total Deliveries, Average Conversion Factor =				27875	0.9847

---------------------------------- Delivery Quarter=1987Q3 ----------------------------------

OBS	Date	Coupon	Maturity	Number Delivered	Factor
30	870930	7.25	5/15/16	4428	0.9163
31	870929	7.25	5/15/16	20	0.9163
32	870924	7.25	5/15/16	1	0.9163
33	870923	7.25	5/15/16	4	0.9163
Total Deliveries, Average Conversion Factor =				4453	0.9163

---------------------------------- Delivery Quarter=1987Q2 ----------------------------------

OBS	Date	Coupon	Maturity	Number Delivered	Factor
34	870630	12.00	8/15/13-08	5913	1.4037
35	870630	12.50	8/15/14-09	900	1.4623
36	870626	7.25	5/15/16	5	0.9159
37	870625	12.00	8/15/13-08	5	1.4037
Total Deliveries, Average Conversion Factor =				6823	1.4111

DISCOUNT CORPORATION OF NEW YORK FUTURES
History of CBOT Bond Deliveries, December 1977 To June 1988

2

------ Delivery Quarter=1987Q1 ------

OBS	Date	Coupon	Maturity	Number Delivered	Factor
38	870331	14.000	11/15/11-06	3484	1.5875
39	870331	12.750	11/15/10-05	2894	1.4546
40	870331	12.000	8/15/13-08	1293	1.4053
41	870331	13.875	5/15/11-06	1227	1.5689
42	870331	13.250	5/15/14-09	1212	1.5394
43	870331	11.750	11/15/14-09	2	1.3885
44	870331	12.500	8/15/14-09	2	1.4640
45	870330	12.750	11/15/10-05	1039	1.4546
46	870330	14.000	11/15/11-06	670	1.5875
47	870330	13.250	5/15/14-09	293	1.5394
48	870330	13.875	5/15/11-06	208	1.5689
49	870327	12.750	11/15/10-05	1400	1.4546
50	870327	14.000	11/15/11-06	581	1.5875
51	870327	13.875	5/15/11-06	120	1.5689
52	870326	12.750	11/15/10-05	1	1.4546
53	870326	14.000	11/15/11-06	1	1.5875
54	870325	12.750	11/15/10-05	1	1.4546

Total Deliveries, Average Conversion Factor = 14428   1.5150

------ Delivery Quarter=1986Q4 ------

OBS	Date	Coupon	Maturity	Number Delivered	Factor
55	861231	14.000	11/15/11-06	3804	1.5903
56	861231	13.875	5/15/11-06	1788	1.5718
57	861231	13.250	5/15/14-09	756	1.5414
58	861231	12.000	8/15/13-08	2	1.4074
59	861231	12.750	11/15/10-05	2	1.4570
60	861230	14.000	11/15/11-06	430	1.5903
61	861230	13.875	5/15/11-06	70	1.5718
62	861230	13.250	5/15/14-09	2	1.5414
63	861223	14.000	11/15/11-06	30	1.5903

Total Deliveries, Average Conversion Factor = 6884   1.5798

------ Delivery Quarter=1986Q3 ------

OBS	Date	Coupon	Maturity	Number Delivered	Factor
64	860930	12.500	8/15/14-09	3792	1.4678
65	860930	13.250	5/15/14-09	761	1.5439
66	860930	14.000	11/15/11-06	15	1.5938
67	860926	12.000	8/15/13-08	1	1.4089
68	860925	12.750	11/15/10-05	2	1.4600
69	860919	14.000	11/15/11-06	2	1.5938
70	860916	7.625	2/15/07-02	4	0.9671
71	860911	14.000	11/15/11-06	2	1.5938
72	860908	12.000	8/15/13-08	7	1.4089

Total Deliveries, Average Conversion Factor = 4586   1.4801

------ Delivery Quarter=1986Q2 ------

OBS	Date	Coupon	Maturity	Number Delivered	Factor
73	860630	12.000	8/15/13-08	3003	1.4110
74	860630	10.375	11/15/12-07	1390	1.2406
75	860630	12.500	8/15/14-09	1001	1.4699
76	860630	12.750	11/15/10-05	520	1.4623
77	860630	14.000	11/15/11-06	95	1.5965
78	860630	11.125	8/15/03	30	1.2877
79	860630	11.750	11/15/14-09	5	1.3928
80	860626	12.000	8/15/13-08	1	1.4110
81	860624	12.000	8/15/13-08	1	1.4110
82	860623	12.500	8/15/14-09	2	1.4699
83	860618	14.000	11/15/11-06	42	1.5965
84	860618	12.500	8/15/14-09	10	1.4699
85	860617	14.000	11/15/11-06	16	1.5965
86	860617	12.500	8/15/14-09	6	1.4699
87	860617	12.750	11/15/10-05	2	1.4623
88	860617	13.250	5/15/14-09	1	1.5458
89	860610	14.000	11/15/11-06	18	1.5965
90	860610	12.500	8/15/14-09	6	1.4699

DISCOUNT CORPORATION OF NEW YORK FUTURES
History of CBOT Bond Deliveries, December 1977 To June 1988

————————————————— Delivery Quarter=1986Q2 —————————————————

OBS	Date	Coupon	Maturity	Number Delivered	Factor
91	860610	13.250	5/15/14-09	5	1.5458
92	860610	12.750	11/15/10-05	3	1.4623
93	860610	12.000	8/15/13-08	1	1.4110
94	860606	12.500	8/15/14-09	1	1.4699
95	860604	12.500	8/15/14-09	92	1.4699
96	860604	14.000	11/15/11-06	83	1.5965
97	860604	13.250	5/15/14-09	27	1.5458
98	860604	8.750	11/15/08-03	1	1.0693
99	860603	13.250	5/15/14-09	36	1.5458
100	860603	14.000	11/15/11-06	36	1.5965
101	860603	12.500	8/15/14-09	18	1.4699
102	860603	13.875	5/15/11-06	2	1.5780
103	860602	14.000	11/15/11-06	1057	1.5965
104	860602	12.750	11/15/10-05	845	1.4623
105	860602	13.250	5/15/14-09	360	1.5458
106	860602	13.875	5/15/11-06	130	1.5780

Total Deliveries, Average Conversion Factor = 8846   1.4365

————————————————— Delivery Quarter=1986Q1 —————————————————

OBS	Date	Coupon	Maturity	Number Delivered	Factor
107	860331	10.375	11/15/12-07	2975	1.2419
108	860331	10.750	5/15/03	2045	1.2532
109	860331	12.750	11/15/10-05	656	1.4651
110	860331	10.000	5/15/10-05	647	1.1937
111	860331	12.000	8/15/13-08	501	1.4124
112	860331	12.500	8/15/14-09	305	1.4714
113	860331	11.750	11/15/14-09	265	1.3946
114	860331	10.750	2/15/03	210	1.2511
115	860331	14.000	11/15/11-06	90	1.5998
116	860331	13.875	5/15/11-06	70	1.5814
117	860331	10.750	8/15/05	60	1.2675
118	860331	11.875	11/15/03	4	1.3616
119	860331	13.250	5/15/14-09	2	1.5482
120	860331	11.250	2/15/15	1	1.3634
121	860324	10.625	8/15/15	4	1.2948
122	860321	12.000	8/15/13-08	4	1.4124
123	860321	14.000	11/15/11-06	2	1.5998
124	860320	14.000	11/15/11-06	102	1.5998
125	860320	12.000	8/15/13-08	7	1.4124
126	860320	12.500	8/15/14-09	6	1.4714
127	860320	11.750	11/15/14-09	3	1.3946
128	860320	12.750	11/15/10-05	3	1.4651
129	860320	13.875	5/15/11-06	3	1.5814
130	860319	12.000	8/15/13-08	2000	1.4124
131	860319	13.250	5/15/14-09	1850	1.5482
132	860319	14.000	11/15/11-06	640	1.5998
133	860319	11.750	11/15/14-09	619	1.3946
134	860319	13.875	5/15/11-06	280	1.5814
135	860319	12.500	8/15/14-09	211	1.4714
136	860318	12.000	8/15/13-08	31	1.4124
137	860314	12.000	8/15/13-08	74	1.4124
138	860314	13.875	5/15/11-06	50	1.5814
139	860312	14.000	11/15/11-06	58	1.5998
140	860312	12.375	5/15/04	45	1.4136
141	860312	14.000	11/15/11-06	18	1.5998
142	860312	13.250	8/15/14-09	9	1.5500
143	860305	8.750	11/15/08-03	1	1.0700
144	860304	7.875	11/15/07-02	10	0.9887
145	860304	7.625	2/15/07-02	10	0.9666
146	860304	11.250	2/15/15	6	1.3634
147	860304	8.750	11/15/08-03	5	1.0700

Total Deliveries, Average Conversion Factor = 13882   1.3773

DISCOUNT CORPORATION OF NEW YORK FUTURES
History of CBOT Bond Deliveries, December 1977 To June 1988

──────────────────── Delivery Quarter=1985Q4 ────────────────────

OBS	Date	Coupon	Maturity	Number Delivered	Factor
148	851231	12.50	8/15/14-09	7155	1.4735
149	851231	12.00	8/15/13-08	5288	1.4144
150	851231	11.75	11/15/14-09	2281	1.3957
151	851231	13.25	5/15/14-09	111	1.5500
152	851231	11.25	2/15/15	11	1.3645
153	851227	12.50	8/15/14-09	110	1.4735
154	851227	12.00	8/15/13-08	70	1.4144
155	851227	13.25	5/15/14-09	70	1.5500
156	851224	12.50	8/15/14-09	4	1.4735

Total Deliveries, Average Conversion Factor = 15100   1.4416

──────────────────── Delivery Quarter=1985Q3 ────────────────────

OBS	Date	Coupon	Maturity	Number Delivered	Factor
157	850930	7.625	2/15/07-02	3263	0.9660
158	850930	10.375	11/15/12-07	2056	1.2440
159	850930	11.750	11/15/14-09	921	1.3974
160	850930	12.500	8/15/14-09	901	1.4749
161	850927	12.500	8/15/14-09	200	1.4749

Total Deliveries, Average Conversion Factor = 7341   1.1743

──────────────────── Delivery Quarter=1985Q2 ────────────────────

OBS	Date	Coupon	Maturity	Number Delivered	Factor
162	850628	11.250	2/15/15	7852	1.3661
163	850628	12.000	8/15/13-08	4016	1.4177
164	850628	12.500	8/15/14-09	782	1.4769
165	850628	10.375	11/15/12-07	2	1.2448
166	850627	11.250	2/15/15	799	1.3661
167	850627	12.000	8/15/13-08	514	1.4177
168	850627	10.375	11/15/09-04	3	1.2310
169	850626	11.250	2/15/15	1	1.3661
170	850625	11.250	2/15/15	376	1.3661
171	850625	12.500	8/15/14-09	300	1.4769
172	850624	11.250	2/15/15	51	1.3661
173	850620	9.125	5/15/09-04	1	1.1081
174	850619	9.125	5/15/09-04	2	1.1081
175	850619	7.625	2/15/07-02	2	0.9660
176	850610	11.250	2/15/15	36	1.3661
177	850607	11.250	2/15/15	2	1.3661
178	850606	11.250	2/15/15	12	1.3661
179	850605	11.250	2/15/15	11	1.3661
180	850604	11.250	2/15/15	58	1.3661
181	850603	11.250	2/15/15	60	1.3661

Total Deliveries, Average Conversion Factor = 14880   1.3900

──────────────────── Delivery Quarter=1985Q1 ────────────────────

OBS	Date	Coupon	Maturity	Number Delivered	Factor
182	850329	7.625	2/15/07-02	4747	0.9655
183	850329	7.875	11/15/07-02	692	0.9883
184	850329	11.250	2/15/15	1	1.3666
185	850328	7.625	2/15/07-02	417	0.9655
186	850328	11.625	11/15/02	1	1.3383
187	850327	7.625	2/15/07-02	755	0.9655
188	850327	8.750	11/15/08-03	8	1.0718
189	850326	7.875	11/15/07-02	1	0.9883

Total Deliveries, Average Conversion Factor = 6622   0.9681

DISCOUNT CORPORATION OF NEW YORK FUTURES
History of CBOT Bond Deliveries, December 1977 To June 1988

5

───────────────── Delivery Quarter=1984Q4 ─────────────────

OBS	Date	Coupon	Maturity	Number Delivered	Factor
190	841231	10.375	11/15/12-07	11519	1.2468
191	841231	12.000	8/15/13-08	3398	1.4209
192	841231	7.625	2/15/07-02	3290	0.9655
193	841231	12.500	8/15/14-09	3130	1.4802
194	841231	8.750	11/15/08-03	821	1.0720
195	841231	7.875	11/15/07-02	298	0.9881
196	841231	8.375	8/15/08-03	8	1.0359
197	841228	7.625	2/15/07-02	1302	0.9655
198	841228	10.375	11/15/12-07	1210	1.2468
199	841228	8.750	11/15/08-03	380	1.0720
200	841228	12.500	8/15/14-09	200	1.4802
201	841228	7.875	11/15/07-02	157	0.9881
202	841228	12.000	8/15/13-08	70	1.4209
203	841227	7.625	2/15/07-02	10	0.9655
204	841226	7.625	2/15/07-02	9	0.9655
205	841226	8.750	11/15/08-03	3	1.0720
206	841226	10.375	11/15/12-07	2	1.2468
207	841221	10.375	11/15/12-07	15	1.2468
208	841220	10.375	11/15/12-07	467	1.2468
209	841220	7.625	2/15/07-02	3	0.9655
210	841217	7.625	2/15/07-02	25	0.9655
211	841214	7.625	2/15/07-02	16	0.9655
212	841213	7.625	2/15/07-02	50	0.9655

Total Deliveries, Average Conversion Factor = 26383   1.2365

───────────────── Delivery Quarter=1984Q3 ─────────────────

OBS	Date	Coupon	Maturity	Number Delivered	Factor
213	840928	7.625	2/15/07-02	6979	0.9651
214	840928	10.375	11/15/12-07	4495	1.2480
215	840928	8.750	11/15/08-03	2260	1.0726
216	840928	7.875	11/15/07-02	1250	0.9882
217	840928	8.375	8/15/08-03	138	1.0359
218	840928	9.125	5/15/09-04	130	1.1102
219	840927	10.375	11/15/12-07	1489	1.2480
220	840927	7.625	2/15/07-02	701	0.9651
221	840927	7.875	11/15/07-02	265	0.9882
222	840926	10.375	11/15/12-07	242	1.2480
223	840926	7.875	11/15/07-02	113	0.9882
224	840925	7.625	2/15/07-02	120	0.9651
225	840925	10.375	11/15/12-07	30	1.2480
226	840925	8.750	11/15/08-03	1	1.0726
227	840924	10.375	11/15/12-07	2787	1.2480
228	840924	9.125	5/15/09-04	1	1.1102
229	840921	7.625	2/15/07-02	10	0.9651
230	840920	10.375	11/15/12-07	1	1.2480
231	840919	7.625	2/15/07-02	1	0.9651
232	840911	7.625	2/15/07-02	1	0.9651
233	840907	7.625	2/15/07-02	1	0.9651
234	840906	8.750	11/15/08-03	30	1.0726
235	840906	7.625	2/15/07-02	1	0.9651
236	840905	7.625	2/15/07-02	1	0.9651
237	840904	7.625	2/15/07-02	1	0.9651

Total Deliveries, Average Conversion Factor = 21048   1.1015

───────────────── Delivery Quarter=1984Q2 ─────────────────

OBS	Date	Coupon	Maturity	Number Delivered	Factor
238	840629	8.750	11/15/08-03	5131	1.0728
239	840629	7.625	2/15/07-02	4734	0.9650
240	840629	7.625	11/15/07-02	1091	0.9641
241	840629	10.375	11/15/12-07	524	1.2487
242	840629	8.375	8/15/08-03	80	1.0363
243	840628	8.750	11/15/08-03	4407	1.0728
244	840628	7.625	2/15/07-02	3435	0.9650
245	840628	7.875	11/15/07-02	158	0.9879
246	840606	8.375	8/15/08-03	1	1.0363
247	840605	8.375	8/15/08-03	1	1.0363

Total Deliveries, Average Conversion Factor = 19562   1.0256

DISCOUNT CORPORATION OF NEW YORK FUTURES
History of CBOT Bond Deliveries, December 1977 To June 1988

---------------------------- Delivery Quarter=1984Q1 ----------------------------

OBS	Date	Coupon	Maturity	Number Delivered	Factor
248	840330	10.375	11/15/12-07	5731	1.2499
249	840330	7.625	2/15/07-02	5123	0.9646
250	840330	8.750	11/15/08-03	3978	1.0734
251	840330	7.875	11/15/07-02	478	0.9880
252	840330	9.125	5/15/09-04	270	1.1113
253	840329	7.625	2/15/07-02	100	0.9646
254	840328	8.750	11/15/08-03	2	1.0734
255	840327	8.750	11/15/08-03	2	1.0734
256	840326	7.625	2/15/07-02	10	0.9646
257	840322	8.750	11/15/08-03	461	1.0734
258	840322	7.625	2/15/07-02	35	0.9646
259	840321	7.625	2/15/07-02	500	0.9646
260	840320	7.625	2/15/07-02	12	0.9646
261	840320	8.750	11/15/08-03	2	1.0734
262	840319	7.625	2/15/07-02	1	0.9646
263	840316	8.750	11/15/08-03	127	1.0734
264	840316	7.625	2/15/07-02	88	0.9646
265	840315	7.625	2/15/07-02	960	0.9646
266	840315	8.750	11/15/08-03	390	1.0734
267	840314	7.875	11/15/07-02	5	0.9880
268	840313	7.875	11/15/07-02	1	0.9880
269	840312	7.875	11/15/07-02	10	0.9880

Total Deliveries, Average Conversion Factor = 18286   1.0863

---------------------------- Delivery Quarter=1983Q4 ----------------------------

OBS	Date	Coupon	Maturity	Number Delivered	Factor
270	831230	8.750	11/15/08-03	1426	1.0736
271	831230	7.625	2/15/07-02	1126	0.9645
272	831230	10.375	11/15/12-07	107	1.2505
273	831230	7.875	11/15/07-02	13	0.9878
274	831223	10.375	11/15/12-07	2	1.2505
275	831222	8.750	11/15/08-03	90	1.0736
276	831221	8.750	11/15/08-03	145	1.0736
277	831220	8.750	11/15/08-03	1314	1.0736
278	831219	8.750	11/15/08-03	50	1.0736
279	831216	8.750	11/15/08-03	19	1.0736
280	831215	8.750	11/15/08-03	68	1.0736

Total Deliveries, Average Conversion Factor = 4360   1.0496

---------------------------- Delivery Quarter=1983Q3 ----------------------------

OBS	Date	Coupon	Maturity	Number Delivered	Factor
281	830930	8.750	11/15/08-03	2255	1.0742
282	830930	7.625	2/15/07-02	1396	0.9641
283	830930	9.125	5/15/09-04	482	1.1125
284	830930	7.875	11/15/07-02	227	0.9879
285	830930	12.000	8/15/13-08	123	1.4280
286	830929	7.625	2/15/07-02	333	0.9641
287	830929	7.875	11/15/07-02	118	0.9879
288	830929	8.750	11/15/08-03	10	1.0742
289	830923	8.750	11/15/08-03	4	1.0742
290	830922	8.750	11/15/08-03	26	1.0742
291	830922	10.375	11/15/12-07	2	1.2517
292	830921	8.750	11/15/08-03	59	1.0742
293	830920	8.750	11/15/08-03	116	1.0742
294	830920	10.375	11/15/12-07	50	1.2517
295	830914	14.000	11/15/11-06	6	1.6265

Total Deliveries, Average Conversion Factor = 5207   1.0462

DISCOUNT CORPORATION OF NEW YORK FUTURES   7
History of CBOT Bond Deliveries, December 1977 To June 1988

────────────────── Delivery Quarter=1983Q2 ──────────────────

OBS	Date	Coupon	Maturity	Number Delivered	Factor
296	830630	14.000	11/15/11-06	4764	1.6286
297	830630	13.875	5/15/11-06	317	1.6108
298	830630	12.750	11/15/10-05	181	1.4898
299	830627	13.875	5/15/11-06	3	1.6108
300	830624	14.000	11/15/11-06	200	1.6286
301	830624	12.750	11/15/10-05	1	1.4898
302	830623	14.000	11/15/11-06	22	1.6286
303	830623	13.875	5/15/11-06	1	1.6108
304	830623	9.125	5/15/09-04	1	1.1128
305	830622	14.000	11/15/11-06	1468	1.6286
306	830622	12.750	11/15/10-05	50	1.4898
307	830621	14.000	11/15/11-06	868	1.6286
308	830620	14.000	11/15/11-06	350	1.6286
309	830617	14.000	11/15/11-06	1	1.6286
310	830616	13.875	5/15/11-06	3	1.6108
311	830616	14.000	11/15/11-06	1	1.6286
312	830615	13.875	5/15/11-06	1	1.6108
313	830614	13.875	5/15/11-06	6	1.6108
314	830614	14.000	11/15/11-06	1	1.6286
315	830613	13.875	5/15/11-06	6	1.6108
316	830613	14.000	11/15/11-06	1	1.6286
317	830610	13.875	5/15/11-06	42	1.6108
318	830610	14.000	11/15/11-06	5	1.6286
319	830609	13.875	5/15/11-06	35	1.6108
320	830608	13.875	5/15/11-06	294	1.6108
321	830607	13.875	5/15/11-06	293	1.6108
322	830606	13.875	5/15/11-06	321	1.6108
323	830603	13.875	5/15/11-06	287	1.6108
324	830602	13.875	5/15/11-06	791	1.6108
325	830601	13.875	5/15/11-06	1000	1.6108

Total Deliveries, Average Conversion Factor =   11314   1.6204

────────────────── Delivery Quarter=1983Q1 ──────────────────

OBS	Date	Coupon	Maturity	Number Delivered	Factor
326	830331	12.750	11/15/10-05	850	1.4921
327	830331	14.000	11/15/11-06	420	1.6313
328	830331	13.875	5/15/11-06	24	1.6135
329	830329	13.875	5/15/11-06	1	1.6135
330	830324	13.875	5/15/11-06	3	1.6135
331	830323	14.000	11/15/11-06	213	1.6313
332	830323	13.875	5/15/11-06	71	1.6135
333	830322	14.000	11/15/11-06	6072	1.6313
334	830322	13.875	5/15/11-06	1634	1.6135
335	830322	12.750	11/15/10-05	400	1.4921
336	830321	14.000	11/15/11-06	1	1.6313
337	830318	13.875	5/15/11-06	1061	1.6135
338	830318	14.000	11/15/11-06	282	1.6313
339	830317	14.000	11/15/11-06	942	1.6313
340	830317	13.875	5/15/11-06	686	1.6135

Total Deliveries, Average Conversion Factor =   12660   1.6127

────────────────── Delivery Quarter=1982Q4 ──────────────────

OBS	Date	Coupon	Maturity	Number Delivered	Factor
341	821230	12.750	11/15/10-05	1150	1.4938
342	821230	13.875	5/15/11-06	157	1.6155
343	821229	14.000	11/15/11-06	92	1.6333
344	821228	13.875	5/15/11-06	20	1.6155
345	821227	13.875	5/15/11-06	86	1.6155
346	821223	8.750	11/15/08-03	51	1.0751
347	821222	13.875	5/15/11-06	137	1.6155
348	821222	14.000	11/15/11-06	95	1.6333
349	821221	14.000	11/15/11-06	4917	1.6333
350	821221	13.875	5/15/11-06	4112	1.6155

Total Deliveries, Average Conversion Factor =   10817   1.6084

DISCOUNT CORPORATION OF NEW YORK FUTURES
History of CBOT Bond Deliveries, December 1977 To June 1988

──────────────── Delivery Quarter=1982Q3 ────────────────

OBS	Date	Coupon	Maturity	Number Delivered	Factor
351	820930	8.750	11/15/08-03	7536	1.0757
352	820930	9.125	5/15/09-04	4893	1.1146
353	820930	8.375	8/15/08-03	95	1.0375
354	820930	13.125	5/15/01	1	1.4905
355	820927	14.000	11/15/11-06	1	1.6359
356	820927	8.750	11/15/08-03	1	1.0757
357	820924	8.750	11/15/08-03	1	1.0757
358	820923	8.750	11/15/08-03	1	1.0757
359	820920	8.750	11/15/08-03	1	1.0757
360	820910	8.750	11/15/08-03	5	1.0757

Total Deliveries, Average Conversion Factor = 12535   1.0907

──────────────── Delivery Quarter=1982Q2 ────────────────

OBS	Date	Coupon	Maturity	Number Delivered	Factor
361	820630	8.750	11/15/08-03	1275	1.0758
362	820630	10.000	5/15/10-05	87	1.2078
363	820630	9.125	5/15/09-04	2	1.1149
364	820630	8.375	8/15/08-03	1	1.0378
365	820628	8.750	11/15/08-03	5	1.0758
366	820625	8.750	11/15/08-03	7	1.0758
367	820624	8.750	11/15/08-03	7	1.0758
368	820623	8.750	11/15/08-03	19	1.0758
369	820623	10.000	5/15/10-05	6	1.2078
370	820622	10.000	5/15/10-05	1	1.2078
371	820621	8.750	11/15/08-03	19	1.0758
372	820621	10.000	5/15/10-05	5	1.2078
373	820618	8.750	11/15/08-03	20	1.0758
374	820617	10.000	5/15/10-05	4	1.2078
375	820617	9.125	5/15/09-04	2	1.1149
376	820616	10.000	5/15/10-05	5	1.2078
377	820615	10.000	5/15/10-05	30	1.2078
378	820614	10.000	5/15/10-05	51	1.2078
379	820611	10.000	5/15/10-05	345	1.2078
380	820611	9.125	5/15/09-04	14	1.1149
381	820609	10.000	5/15/10-05	5	1.2078
382	820607	9.125	5/15/09-04	2	1.1149
383	820607	10.000	5/15/10-05	1	1.2078
384	820604	9.125	5/15/09-04	2	1.1149
385	820604	8.750	11/15/08-03	2	1.0758
386	820604	10.000	5/15/10-05	1	1.2078
387	820603	9.125	5/15/09-04	2	1.1149
388	820603	8.750	11/15/08-03	2	1.0758
389	820603	10.000	5/15/10-05	1	1.2078
390	820602	8.750	11/15/08-03	2	1.0758
391	820602	9.125	5/15/09-04	2	1.1149
392	820602	10.000	5/15/10-05	1	1.2078
393	820601	9.125	5/15/09-04	3	1.1149
394	820601	8.750	11/15/08-03	2	1.0758
395	820601	10.000	5/15/10-05	1	1.2078

Total Deliveries, Average Conversion Factor = 1934   1.1135

──────────────── Delivery Quarter=1982Q1 ────────────────

OBS	Date	Coupon	Maturity	Number Delivered	Factor
396	820331	10.000	5/15/10-05	1303	1.2088
397	820331	8.750	11/15/08-03	353	1.0764
398	820331	8.375	8/15/08-03	37	1.0378
399	820331	10.375	11/15/09-04	3	1.2461
400	820331	14.000	11/15/11-06	1	1.6402
401	820330	8.750	11/15/08-03	5	1.0764
402	820317	8.750	11/15/08-03	1	1.0764
403	820312	8.750	11/15/08-03	2	1.0764
404	820311	8.750	11/15/08-03	14	1.0764
405	820310	8.750	11/15/08-03	20	1.0764
406	820309	8.750	11/15/08-03	121	1.0764
407	820308	8.750	11/15/08-03	152	1.0764
408	820305	8.750	11/15/08-03	157	1.0764
409	820304	8.750	11/15/08-03	445	1.0764
410	820303	9.125	5/15/09-04	1919	1.1156
411	820303	8.750	11/15/08-03	1367	1.0764

DISCOUNT CORPORATION OF NEW YORK FUTURES
History of CBOT Bond Deliveries, December 1977 To June 1988

9

──────────────── Delivery Quarter=1982Q1 ────────────────

OBS	Date	Coupon	Maturity	Number Delivered	Factor
412	820303	9.125	5/15/09-04	329	1.1156
413	820303	9.125	5/15/09-04	136	1.1156
414	820303	9.125	5/15/09-04	96	1.1156
415	820303	9.125	5/15/09-04	65	1.1156
416	820303	9.125	5/15/09-04	45	1.1156
417	820303	9.125	5/15/09-04	5	1.1156
418	820303	9.125	5/15/09-04	1	1.1156
419	820303	9.125	5/15/09-04	1	1.1156
420	820303	9.125	5/15/09-04	1	1.1156
421	820303	9.125	5/15/09-04	1	1.1156

Total Deliveries, Average Conversion Factor = 6580   1.1181

──────────────── Delivery Quarter=1981Q4 ────────────────

OBS	Date	Coupon	Maturity	Number Delivered	Factor
422	811231	8.750	11/15/08-03	1930	1.0765
423	811231	9.125	5/15/09-04	1273	1.1159
424	811231	8.375	8/15/08-03	149	1.0382
425	811231	10.375	11/15/09-04	115	1.2468
426	811231	14.000	11/15/11-06	100	1.6420
427	811231	10.000	5/15/10-05	60	1.2094
428	811231	11.750	11/15/14-09	10	1.4153
429	811231	12.750	11/15/10-05	1	1.5013
430	811230	13.875	5/15/11-06	415	1.6244
431	811230	12.750	11/15/10-05	1	1.5013
432	811223	8.750	11/15/08-03	41	1.0765
433	811222	8.750	11/15/08-03	269	1.0765
434	811208	8.750	11/15/08-03	1	1.0765
435	811207	14.000	11/15/11-06	2	1.6420
436	811204	14.000	11/15/11-06	2	1.6420
437	811203	14.000	11/15/11-06	2	1.6420
438	811202	14.000	11/15/11-06	126	1.6420
439	811202	7.625	2/15/07-02	4	0.9629
440	811202	7.625	2/15/07-02	2	0.9629
441	811202	7.625	2/15/07-02	2	0.9629

Total Deliveries, Average Conversion Factor = 4505   1.1728

──────────────── Delivery Quarter=1981Q3 ────────────────

OBS	Date	Coupon	Maturity	Number Delivered	Factor
442	810930	13.875	5/15/11-06	2247	1.6269
443	810929	7.625	2/15/07-02	2	0.9625
444	810929	13.875	5/15/11-06	2	1.6269
445	810925	13.875	5/15/11-06	74	1.6269
446	810923	8.750	11/15/08-03	3	1.0771
447	810922	8.750	11/15/08-03	157	1.0771
448	810922	9.125	5/15/09-04	3	1.1166
449	810922	8.375	8/15/08-03	1	1.0382
450	810921	8.750	11/15/08-03	15	1.0771
451	810921	10.375	11/15/09-04	6	1.2480
452	810921	7.625	2/15/07-02	1	0.9625
453	810921	8.375	8/15/08-03	1	1.0382
454	810918	8.750	11/15/08-03	15	1.0771
455	810918	10.375	11/15/09-04	3	1.2480
456	810918	8.375	8/15/08-03	1	1.0382
457	810917	8.750	11/15/08-03	9	1.0771
458	810917	10.375	11/15/09-04	5	1.2480
459	810917	8.375	8/15/08-03	1	1.0382
460	810916	8.750	11/15/08-03	10	1.0771
461	810916	8.375	8/15/08-03	1	1.0382
462	810916	10.375	11/15/09-04	1	1.2480
463	810915	8.750	11/15/08-03	319	1.0771
464	810915	10.375	11/15/09-04	192	1.2480
465	810915	8.375	8/15/08-03	1	1.0382
466	810915	9.125	5/15/09-04	1	1.1166
467	810914	10.375	11/15/09-04	6	1.2480
468	810914	8.750	11/15/08-03	4	1.0771
469	810914	9.125	5/15/09-04	1	1.1166
470	810911	10.375	11/15/09-04	9	1.2480
471	810911	9.125	5/15/09-04	6	1.1166
472	810911	8.750	11/15/08-03	2	1.0771

DISCOUNT CORPORATION OF NEW YORK FUTURES
History of CBOT Bond Deliveries, December 1977 To June 1988

10

----------------------------------- Delivery Quarter=1981Q3 -----------------------------------

OBS	Date	Coupon	Maturity	Number Delivered	Factor
473	810910	10.375	11/15/09-04	22	1.2480
474	810910	8.750	11/15/08-03	12	1.0771
475	810910	9.125	5/15/09-04	8	1.1166
476	810909	10.375	11/15/09-04	15	1.2480
477	810909	8.750	11/15/08-03	11	1.0771
478	810909	9.125	5/15/09-04	7	1.1166
479	810908	8.750	11/15/08-03	9	1.0771
480	810908	10.375	11/15/09-04	8	1.2480
481	810908	9.125	5/15/09-04	6	1.1166
482	810904	8.750	11/15/08-03	25	1.0771
483	810904	10.375	11/15/09-04	19	1.2480
484	810904	9.125	5/15/09-04	15	1.1166
485	810903	10.375	11/15/09-04	53	1.2480
486	810903	8.750	11/15/08-03	39	1.0771
487	810903	9.125	5/15/09-04	20	1.1166
488	810903	8.375	8/15/08-03	14	1.0382
489	810903	7.625	2/15/07-02	5	0.9625
490	810902	10.375	11/15/09-04	125	1.2480
491	810902	8.750	11/15/08-03	95	1.0771
492	810902	7.625	2/15/07-02	30	0.9625
493	810902	8.375	8/15/08-03	30	1.0382
494	810901	7.625	2/15/07-02	30	0.9625

Total Deliveries, Average Conversion Factor = 3697   1.4421

----------------------------------- Delivery Quarter=1981Q2 -----------------------------------

OBS	Date	Coupon	Maturity	Number Delivered	Factor
495	810630	13.875	5/15/11-06	2488	1.6287
496	810630	8.750	11/15/08-03	911	1.0772
497	810630	9.125	5/15/09-04	480	1.1168
498	810630	8.375	8/15/08-03	32	1.0385
499	810630	10.000	5/15/10-05	20	1.2110
500	810630	12.750	11/15/10-05	9	1.5048
501	810626	13.875	5/15/11-06	325	1.6287
502	810625	8.750	11/15/08-03	33	1.0772
503	810622	13.875	5/15/11-06	1	1.6287
504	810619	13.875	5/15/11-06	482	1.6287
505	810619	9.125	5/15/09-04	5	1.1168
506	810619	7.625	2/15/07-02	2	0.9625
507	810618	8.750	11/15/08-03	2	1.0772
508	810618	7.625	2/15/07-02	1	0.9625
509	810618	10.000	5/15/10-05	1	1.2110
510	810617	8.750	11/15/08-03	16	1.0772
511	810617	7.625	2/15/07-02	1	0.9625
512	810612	8.750	11/15/08-03	60	1.0772
513	810612	7.625	2/15/07-02	7	0.9625
514	810611	8.750	11/15/08-03	5	1.0772
515	810611	10.000	5/15/10-05	1	1.2110
516	810610	8.750	11/15/08-03	216	1.0772
517	810610	9.125	5/15/09-04	10	1.1168
518	810610	8.375	8/15/08-03	3	1.0385
519	810609	8.750	11/15/08-03	12	1.0772
520	810609	9.125	5/15/09-04	4	1.1168
521	810609	8.375	8/15/08-03	2	1.0385
522	810609	7.625	2/15/07-02	1	0.9625
523	810608	8.750	11/15/08-03	45	1.0772
524	810608	7.625	2/15/07-02	6	0.9625
525	810608	9.125	5/15/09-04	1	1.1168
526	810608	8.375	8/15/08-03	1	1.0385
527	810605	8.750	11/15/08-03	188	1.0772
528	810605	7.625	2/15/07-02	163	0.9625
529	810605	8.375	8/15/08-03	20	1.0385
530	810605	9.125	5/15/09-04	14	1.1168
531	810604	8.750	11/15/08-03	245	1.0772
532	810604	7.625	2/15/07-02	105	0.9625
533	810604	8.375	8/15/08-03	26	1.0385
534	810604	9.125	5/15/09-04	11	1.1168
535	810603	8.750	11/15/08-03	686	1.0772
536	810603	7.625	2/15/07-02	254	0.9625
537	810603	9.125	5/15/09-04	55	1.1168
538	810603	8.375	8/15/08-03	30	1.0385
539	810602	8.750	11/15/08-03	1024	1.0772
540	810602	7.625	2/15/07-02	400	0.9625
541	810602	8.375	8/15/08-03	46	1.0385

DISCOUNT CORPORATION OF NEW YORK FUTURES
History of CBOT Bond Deliveries, December 1977 To June 1988

11

────────────────────── Delivery Quarter=1981Q2 ──────────────────────

OBS	Date	Coupon	Maturity	Number Delivered	Factor
542	810602	9.125	5/15/09-04	22	1.1168
543	810601	12.750	11/15/10-05	11	1.5048

Total Deliveries, Average Conversion Factor = 8483   1.2822

────────────────────── Delivery Quarter=1981Q1 ──────────────────────

OBS	Date	Coupon	Maturity	Number Delivered	Factor
544	810331	12.750	11/15/10-05	2092	1.5069
545	810326	12.750	11/15/10-05	15	1.5069
546	810325	12.750	11/15/10-05	103	1.5069
547	810323	12.750	11/15/10-05	2	1.5069
548	810323	7.625	2/15/07-02	1	0.9621
549	810320	12.750	11/15/10-05	2	1.5069
550	810319	12.750	11/15/10-05	11	1.5069
551	810319	7.625	2/15/07-02	1	0.9621
552	810319	8.375	8/15/08-03	1	1.0385
553	810318	12.750	11/15/10-05	34	1.5069
554	810318	11.750	11/15/14-09	1	1.4186
555	810317	8.750	11/15/08-03	352	1.0777
556	810317	12.750	11/15/10-05	165	1.5069
557	810317	8.375	8/15/08-03	78	1.0385
558	810317	7.625	2/15/07-02	2	0.9621
559	810316	8.750	11/15/08-03	1	1.0777
560	810313	8.750	11/15/08-03	2	1.0777
561	810311	7.625	2/15/07-02	1	0.9621
562	810310	8.750	11/15/08-03	3	1.0777
563	810310	8.375	8/15/08-03	2	1.0385
564	810306	8.750	11/15/08-03	88	1.0777
565	810306	12.750	11/15/10-05	8	1.5069
566	810306	8.375	8/15/08-03	2	1.0385
567	810305	8.750	11/15/08-03	76	1.0777
568	810305	8.375	8/15/08-03	5	1.0385
569	810305	7.625	2/15/07-02	5	0.9621
570	810305	12.750	11/15/10-05	2	1.5069
571	810304	8.750	11/15/08-03	108	1.0777
572	810304	12.750	11/15/10-05	53	1.5069
573	810304	8.375	8/15/08-03	24	1.0385
574	810304	9.125	5/15/09-04	20	1.1175
575	810304	11.750	11/15/14-09	1	1.4186
576	810303	8.750	11/15/08-03	162	1.0777
577	810303	12.750	11/15/10-05	102	1.5069
578	810303	8.375	8/15/08-03	59	1.0385
579	810303	9.125	5/15/09-04	40	1.1175
580	810303	7.625	2/15/07-02	21	0.9621
581	810303	11.750	11/15/14-09	2	1.4186
582	810302	8.750	11/15/08-03	433	1.0777
583	810302	8.375	8/15/08-03	80	1.0385
584	810302	9.125	5/15/09-04	40	1.1175
585	810302	7.625	2/15/07-02	21	0.9621
586	810302	12.750	11/15/10-05	2	1.5069
587	810302	11.750	11/15/14-09	2	1.4186

Total Deliveries, Average Conversion Factor = 4225   1.3386

────────────────────── Delivery Quarter=1980Q4 ──────────────────────

OBS	Date	Coupon	Maturity	Number Delivered	Factor
588	801231	7.625	2/15/07-02	135	0.9622
589	801231	8.750	11/15/08-03	6	1.0778
590	801230	7.625	2/15/07-02	2602	0.9622
591	801229	8.750	11/15/08-03	8	1.0778
592	801224	7.625	2/15/07-02	2000	0.9622
593	801224	12.750	11/15/10-05	2	1.5082
594	801222	8.750	11/15/08-03	8	1.0778
595	801222	8.375	8/15/08-03	2	1.0389
596	801219	9.125	5/15/09-04	35	1.1177
597	801219	8.750	11/15/08-03	28	1.0778
598	801219	8.375	8/15/08-03	11	1.0389
599	801219	12.750	11/15/10-05	7	1.5082
600	801218	8.750	11/15/08-03	1	1.0778
601	801217	8.750	11/15/08-03	1	1.0778
602	801216	8.750	11/15/08-03	601	1.0778

DISCOUNT CORPORATION OF NEW YORK FUTURES
History of CBOT Bond Deliveries, December 1977 To June 1988

——————————————————————————————— Delivery Quarter=1980Q4 ———————————————————————————————

OBS	Date	Coupon	Maturity	Number Delivered	Factor
603	801216	9.125	5/15/09-04	8	1.1177
604	801216	8.375	8/15/08-03	1	1.0389
605	801215	8.375	8/15/08-03	53	1.0389
606	801215	8.750	11/15/08-03	51	1.0778
607	801212	8.750	11/15/08-03	453	1.0778
608	801212	8.375	8/15/08-03	23	1.0389
609	801212	12.750	11/15/10-05	1	1.5082
610	801212	9.125	5/15/09-04	1	1.1177
611	801211	8.750	11/15/08-03	115	1.0778
612	801211	12.750	11/15/10-05	17	1.5082
613	801211	8.375	8/15/08-03	14	1.0389
614	801211	9.125	5/15/09-04	6	1.1177
615	801210	8.750	11/15/08-03	291	1.0778
616	801210	9.125	5/15/09-04	86	1.1177
617	801210	8.375	8/15/08-03	45	1.0389
618	801210	12.750	11/15/10-05	24	1.5082
619	801209	8.750	11/15/08-03	492	1.0778
620	801209	12.750	11/15/10-05	162	1.5082
621	801209	9.125	5/15/09-04	133	1.1177
622	801209	8.375	8/15/08-03	58	1.0389
623	801208	8.750	11/15/08-03	32	1.0778
624	801208	8.375	8/15/08-03	1	1.0389
625	801205	8.750	11/15/08-03	67	1.0778
626	801205	8.375	8/15/08-03	6	1.0389
627	801204	8.375	8/15/08-03	42	1.0389
628	801204	8.750	11/15/08-03	30	1.0778
629	801203	8.750	11/15/08-03	129	1.0778
630	801203	8.375	8/15/08-03	32	1.0389
631	801203	11.750	11/15/14-09	2	1.4193
632	801202	8.750	11/15/08-03	502	1.0778
633	801202	8.375	8/15/08-03	140	1.0389
634	801201	8.750	11/15/08-03	41	1.0778
635	801201	11.750	11/15/14-09	1	1.4193

Total Deliveries, Average Conversion Factor = 8506   1.0236

——————————————————————————————— Delivery Quarter=1980Q3 ———————————————————————————————

OBS	Date	Coupon	Maturity	Number Delivered	Factor
636	800930	11.75	11/15/14-09	3233	1.4206
637	800929	11.75	11/15/14-09	1	1.4206
638	800926	11.75	11/15/14-09	1	1.4206
639	800925	11.75	11/15/14-09	1	1.4206
640	800924	11.75	11/15/14-09	3	1.4206
641	800923	11.75	11/15/14-09	1	1.4206
642	800922	11.75	11/15/14-09	1	1.4206
643	800919	11.75	11/15/14-09	3	1.4206
644	800917	11.75	11/15/14-09	14	1.4206
645	800916	11.75	11/15/14-09	346	1.4206

Total Deliveries, Average Conversion Factor = 3604   1.4206

——————————————————————————————— Delivery Quarter=1980Q2 ———————————————————————————————

OBS	Date	Coupon	Maturity	Number Delivered	Factor
646	800630	11.750	11/15/14-09	3554	1.4212
647	800630	8.750	11/15/08-03	1	1.0784
648	800627	11.750	11/15/14-09	1055	1.4212
649	800626	11.750	11/15/14-09	23	1.4212
650	800626	8.375	8/15/08-03	5	1.0392
651	800626	11.250	5/15/05-00	3	1.3197
652	800625	9.125	5/15/09-04	5	1.1186
653	800625	11.750	11/15/14-09	5	1.4212
654	800624	11.750	11/15/14-09	357	1.4212
655	800620	11.750	11/15/14-09	34	1.4212
656	800619	11.750	11/15/14-09	11	1.4212
657	800618	11.750	11/15/14-09	4	1.4212
658	800617	11.750	11/15/14-09	675	1.4212
659	800613	11.750	11/15/14-09	10	1.4212
660	800612	11.750	11/15/14-09	12	1.4212
661	800612	8.750	11/15/08-03	1	1.0784
662	800611	11.750	11/15/14-09	6	1.4212
663	800610	11.750	11/15/14-09	400	1.4212

DISCOUNT CORPORATION OF NEW YORK FUTURES

13

History of CBOT Bond Deliveries, December 1977 To June 1988

--------------------------------- Delivery Quarter=1980Q2 ---------------------------------

OBS	Date	Coupon	Maturity	Number Delivered	Factor
664	800603	8.750	11/15/08-03	1	1.0784
665	800602	8.375	8/15/08-03	49	1.0392
666	800602	8.750	11/15/08-03	26	1.0784
667	800602	11.250	5/15/05-00	4	1.3197

Total Deliveries, Average Conversion Factor = 6241   1.4160

--------------------------------- Delivery Quarter=1980Q1 ---------------------------------

OBS	Date	Coupon	Maturity	Number Delivered	Factor
668	800326	8.750	11/15/08-03	93	1.0789
669	800325	8.750	11/15/08-03	35	1.0789
670	800324	8.375	8/15/08-03	12	1.0391
671	800320	8.750	11/15/08-03	781	1.0789
672	800320	8.250	5/15/05-00	4	1.0247
673	800319	8.750	11/15/08-03	46	1.0789
674	800319	9.125	5/15/09-04	2	1.1192
675	800317	8.750	11/15/08-03	92	1.0789
676	800317	9.125	5/15/09-04	10	1.1192
677	800314	8.750	11/15/08-03	77	1.0789
678	800314	8.375	8/15/08-03	33	1.0391
679	800313	8.750	11/15/08-03	561	1.0789
680	800313	8.375	8/15/08-03	46	1.0391
681	800313	8.250	5/15/05-00	29	1.0247
682	800312	9.125	5/15/09-04	10	1.1192
683	800312	8.750	11/15/08-03	7	1.0789
684	800311	8.750	11/15/08-03	99	1.0789
685	800310	8.375	8/15/08-03	148	1.0391
686	800310	8.750	11/15/08-03	147	1.0789
687	800310	8.000	8/15/01-96	75	0.9998
688	800310	8.250	5/15/05-00	35	1.0247
689	800310	9.125	5/15/09-04	15	1.1192
690	800310	7.625	2/15/07-02	14	0.9615
691	800307	8.375	8/15/08-03	30	1.0391
692	800307	8.750	11/15/08-03	21	1.0789
693	800306	8.750	11/15/08-03	56	1.0789
694	800306	8.375	8/15/08-03	7	1.0391
695	800306	7.625	2/15/07-02	1	0.9615
696	800305	8.750	11/15/08-03	145	1.0789
697	800305	8.375	8/15/08-03	60	1.0391
698	800305	7.625	2/15/07-02	14	0.9615
699	800305	8.250	5/15/05-00	10	1.0247
700	800305	9.125	5/15/09-04	2	1.1192
701	800305	8.000	8/15/01-96	2	0.9998
702	800304	8.750	11/15/08-03	792	1.0789
703	800304	8.375	8/15/08-03	247	1.0391
704	800304	9.125	5/15/09-04	79	1.1192
705	800304	8.000	8/15/01-96	76	0.9998
706	800304	8.250	5/15/05-00	55	1.0247
707	800304	7.625	2/15/07-02	15	0.9615
708	800303	8.375	8/15/08-03	145	1.0391
709	800303	8.750	11/15/08-03	98	1.0789

Total Deliveries, Average Conversion Factor = 4226   1.0674

--------------------------------- Delivery Quarter=1979Q4 ---------------------------------

OBS	Date	Coupon	Maturity	Number Delivered	Factor
710	791228	8.750	11/15/08-03	45	1.0790
711	791227	8.750	11/15/08-03	91	1.0790
712	791227	9.125	5/15/09-04	21	1.1194
713	791227	8.375	8/15/08-03	10	1.0395
714	791221	8.375	8/15/08-03	60	1.0395
715	791221	8.750	11/15/08-03	40	1.0790
716	791220	8.750	11/15/08-03	100	1.0790
717	791217	8.250	5/15/05-00	20	1.0247
718	791214	8.375	8/15/08-03	120	1.0395
719	791214	8.750	11/15/08-03	16	1.0790
720	791213	8.375	8/15/08-03	79	1.0395
721	791212	8.750	11/15/08-03	349	1.0790
722	791212	8.375	8/15/08-03	304	1.0395
723	791211	8.375	8/15/08-03	144	1.0395
724	791210	8.375	8/15/08-03	144	1.0395

DISCOUNT CORPORATION OF NEW YORK FUTURES
History of CBOT Bond Deliveries, December 1977 To June 1988

14

―――――――――――――――――――――― Delivery Quarter=1979Q4 ――――――――――――――――――――――

OBS	Date	Coupon	Maturity	Number Delivered	Factor
725	791207	8.375	8/15/08-03	184	1.0395
726	791206	9.125	5/15/09-04	2	1.1194
727	791204	9.125	5/15/09-04	43	1.1194
728	791204	10.375	11/15/09-04	10	1.2540
729	791204	8.375	8/15/08-03	2	1.0395
730	791204	8.750	11/15/08-03	1	1.0790
731	791203	9.125	5/15/09-04	405	1.1194
732	791203	8.375	8/15/08-03	72	1.0395
733	791203	8.750	11/15/08-03	70	1.0790

Total Deliveries, Average Conversion Factor = 2332   1.0685

―――――――――――――――――――――― Delivery Quarter=1979Q3 ――――――――――――――――――――――

OBS	Date	Coupon	Maturity	Number Delivered	Factor
734	790928	9.125	5/15/09-04	692	1.1200
735	790927	9.125	5/15/09-04	126	1.1200
736	790927	8.750	11/15/08-03	120	1.0795
737	790927	8.375	8/15/08-03	10	1.0394
738	790926	9.125	5/15/09-04	100	1.1200
739	790926	8.750	11/15/08-03	50	1.0795
740	790925	8.375	8/15/08-03	40	1.0394
741	790924	8.375	8/15/08-03	109	1.0394
742	790924	8.750	11/15/08-03	64	1.0795
743	790924	9.125	5/15/09-04	26	1.1200
744	790921	9.125	5/15/09-04	140	1.1200
745	790920	8.750	11/15/08-03	50	1.0795
746	790919	9.125	5/15/09-04	75	1.1200
747	790914	9.125	5/15/09-04	200	1.1200
748	790913	8.750	11/15/08-03	20	1.0795
749	790912	8.750	11/15/08-03	15	1.0795
750	790911	8.750	11/15/08-03	15	1.0795
751	790911	9.125	5/15/09-04	10	1.1200
752	790910	8.750	11/15/08-03	150	1.0795
753	790910	9.125	5/15/09-04	30	1.1200
754	790907	9.125	5/15/09-04	400	1.1200

Total Deliveries, Average Conversion Factor = 2442   1.1067

―――――――――――――――――――――― Delivery Quarter=1979Q2 ――――――――――――――――――――――

OBS	Date	Coupon	Maturity	Number Delivered	Factor
755	790629	9.125	5/15/09-04	155	1.1202
756	790626	9.125	5/15/09-04	2	1.1202
757	790615	9.125	5/15/09-04	40	1.1202
758	790612	9.125	5/15/09-04	4	1.1202
759	790611	9.125	5/15/09-04	20	1.1202
760	790608	7.625	2/15/07-02	20	0.9612
761	790608	9.125	5/15/09-04	10	1.1202
762	790607	9.125	5/15/09-04	130	1.1202
763	790607	7.625	2/15/07-02	40	0.9612
764	790606	9.125	5/15/09-04	150	1.1202
765	790605	9.125	5/15/09-04	58	1.1202
766	790605	7.625	2/15/07-02	10	0.9612
767	790604	9.125	5/15/09-04	414	1.1202
768	790604	7.625	2/15/07-02	105	0.9612
769	790601	9.125	5/15/09-04	637	1.1202
770	790601	7.625	2/15/07-02	546	0.9612

Total Deliveries, Average Conversion Factor = 2341   1.0712

DISCOUNT CORPORATION OF NEW YORK FUTURES   15
History of CBOT Bond Deliveries, December 1977 To June 1988

———————————————— Delivery Quarter=1979Q1 ————————————————

OBS	Date	Coupon	Maturity	Number Delivered	Factor
771	790329	8.750	11/15/08-03	39	1.0800
772	790329	7.625	2/15/07-02	4	0.9608
773	790328	7.625	2/15/07-02	35	0.9608
774	790326	8.750	11/15/08-03	21	1.0800
775	790323	8.750	11/15/08-03	69	1.0800
776	790322	7.625	2/15/07-02	20	0.9608
777	790321	8.750	11/15/08-03	20	1.0800
778	790320	8.750	11/15/08-03	1	1.0800
779	790319	7.625	2/15/07-02	70	0.9608
780	790316	7.625	2/15/07-02	80	0.9608
781	790316	8.750	11/15/08-03	7	1.0800
782	790315	8.750	11/15/08-03	85	1.0800
783	790314	8.750	11/15/08-03	70	1.0800
784	790314	8.250	5/15/05-00	10	1.0252
785	790313	7.625	2/15/07-02	21	0.9608
786	790312	8.750	11/15/08-03	92	1.0800
787	790309	7.625	2/15/07-02	30	0.9608
788	790309	8.375	8/15/08-03	30	1.0397
789	790309	8.750	11/15/08-03	11	1.0800
790	790308	7.625	2/15/07-02	108	0.9608
791	790308	8.750	11/15/08-03	49	1.0800
792	790307	8.750	11/15/08-03	114	1.0800
793	790307	8.375	8/15/08-03	70	1.0397
794	790307	7.625	2/15/07-02	20	0.9608
795	790306	7.625	2/15/07-02	162	0.9608
796	790306	8.750	11/15/08-03	60	1.0800
797	790305	7.625	2/15/07-02	64	0.9608
798	790305	8.750	11/15/08-03	60	1.0800
799	790302	8.750	11/15/08-03	161	1.0800
800	790302	7.625	2/15/07-02	111	0.9608
801	790301	7.625	2/15/07-02	380	0.9608
802	790301	8.750	11/15/08-03	176	1.0800

Total Deliveries, Average Conversion Factor = 2250   1.0194

———————————————— Delivery Quarter=1978Q4 ————————————————

OBS	Date	Coupon	Maturity	Number Delivered	Factor
803	781229	8.375	8/15/08-03	23	1.0400
804	781229	8.750	11/15/08-03	6	1.0801
805	781228	8.750	11/15/08-03	20	1.0801
806	781226	7.625	2/15/07-02	50	0.9608
807	781221	7.625	2/15/07-02	45	0.9608
808	781219	8.750	11/15/08-03	84	1.0801
809	781218	7.625	2/15/07-02	20	0.9608
810	781218	8.750	11/15/08-03	11	1.0801
811	781215	8.750	11/15/08-03	30	1.0801
812	781215	7.625	2/15/07-02	1	0.9608
813	781214	8.750	11/15/08-03	82	1.0801
814	781214	7.625	2/15/07-02	55	0.9608
815	781213	8.750	11/15/08-03	6	1.0801
816	781212	8.750	11/15/08-03	157	1.0801
817	781212	7.625	2/15/07-02	55	0.9608
818	781211	8.750	11/15/08-03	32	1.0801
819	781208	8.750	11/15/08-03	208	1.0801
820	781207	8.750	11/15/08-03	156	1.0801
821	781206	8.750	11/15/08-03	64	1.0801
822	781206	8.375	8/15/08-03	10	1.0400
823	781205	8.750	11/15/08-03	584	1.0801
824	781204	8.750	11/15/08-03	200	1.0801
825	781201	8.750	11/15/08-03	1661	1.0801

Total Deliveries, Average Conversion Factor = 3560   1.0722

DISCOUNT CORPORATION OF NEW YORK FUTURES
History of CBOT Bond Deliveries, December 1977 To June 1988

--------------------------------- Delivery Quarter=1978Q3 ---------------------------------

OBS	Date	Coupon	Maturity	Number Delivered	Factor
826	780929	8.375	8/15/08-03	591	1.0399
827	780928	8.375	8/15/08-03	80	1.0399
828	780927	8.375	8/15/08-03	50	1.0399
829	780925	8.375	8/15/08-03	10	1.0399
830	780922	8.375	8/15/08-03	20	1.0399
831	780921	8.375	8/15/08-03	10	1.0399
832	780919	8.375	8/15/08-03	10	1.0399
833	780913	8.375	8/15/08-03	60	1.0399
834	780912	8.375	8/15/08-03	230	1.0399
835	780911	8.375	8/15/08-03	60	1.0399
836	780908	8.375	8/15/08-03	50	1.0399

Total Deliveries, Average Conversion Factor = 1171   1.0399

--------------------------------- Delivery Quarter=1978Q2 ---------------------------------

OBS	Date	Coupon	Maturity	Number Delivered	Factor
837	780630	7.625	2/15/07-02	1160	0.9605
838	780629	7.625	2/15/07-02	19	0.9605
839	780628	7.625	2/15/07-02	40	0.9605

Total Deliveries, Average Conversion Factor = 1219   0.9605

--------------------------------- Delivery Quarter=1978Q1 ---------------------------------

OBS	Date	Coupon	Maturity	Number Delivered	Factor
840	780331	8.250	5/15/05-00	85	1.0257
841	780331	7.625	2/15/07-02	40	0.9602
842	780331	8.375	8/15/08-03	7	1.0402
843	780330	8.250	5/15/05-00	43	1.0257
844	780322	8.375	8/15/08-03	7	1.0402
845	780303	8.250	5/15/05-00	9	1.0257
846	780303	8.375	8/15/08-03	2	1.0402
847	780303	7.875	11/15/07-02	1	0.9867

Total Deliveries, Average Conversion Factor = 194   1.0132

--------------------------------- Delivery Quarter=1977Q4 ---------------------------------

OBS	Date	Coupon	Maturity	Number Delivered	Factor
848	771230	8.375	8/15/08-03	352	1.0405
849	771230	8.000	8/15/01-96	285	1.0000
850	771230	8.250	5/15/05-00	81	1.0256
851	771230	7.875	11/15/07-02	11	0.9864

Total Deliveries, Average Conversion Factor = 729   1.0222

Appendix II
History of CBOT Note Deliveries
June 1982–June 1988

DISCOUNT CORPORATION OF NEW YORK FUTURES   1
History of CBOT Note Deliveries, June 1982 To June 1988

––––––––––––––––––––––––––––– Delivery Quarter=1988Q2 –––––––––––––––––––––––––––––

OBS	Date	Coupon	Maturity	Number Delivered	Factor
1	880630	8.125	980215	14196	1.0082
2	880630	7.375	960515	52	0.9642
3	880630	8.875	971115	30	1.0562
4	880629	8.125	980215	20	1.0082

Total Deliveries, Average Conversion Factor = 14298   1.0081

––––––––––––––––––––––––––––– Delivery Quarter=1988Q1 –––––––––––––––––––––––––––––

OBS	Date	Coupon	Maturity	Number Delivered	Factor
5	880331	8.875	971115	4177	1.0575

––––––––––––––––––––––––––––– Delivery Quarter=1987Q4 –––––––––––––––––––––––––––––

OBS	Date	Coupon	Maturity	Number Delivered	Factor
6	871231	8.625	970815	3111	1.0410
7	871230	7.250	961115	350	0.9533

Total Deliveries, Average Conversion Factor = 3461   1.0321

––––––––––––––––––––––––––––– Delivery Quarter=1987Q3 –––––––––––––––––––––––––––––

OBS	Date	Coupon	Maturity	Number Delivered	Factor
8	870930	7.25	961115	9234	0.9525
9	870930	8.50	970515	3448	1.0328
10	870929	7.25	961115	100	0.9525

Total Deliveries, Average Conversion Factor = 12782   0.9742

––––––––––––––––––––––––––––– Delivery Quarter=1987Q2 –––––––––––––––––––––––––––––

OBS	Date	Coupon	Maturity	Number Delivered	Factor
11	870630	7.250	961115	8802	0.9515
12	870630	7.375	960515	648	0.9610

Total Deliveries, Average Conversion Factor = 9450   0.9522

––––––––––––––––––––––––––––– Delivery Quarter=1987Q1 –––––––––––––––––––––––––––––

OBS	Date	Coupon	Maturity	Number Delivered	Factor
13	870331	11.750	931115	3760	1.1872
14	870331	13.125	940515	260	1.2707

Total Deliveries, Average Conversion Factor = 4020   1.1926

––––––––––––––––––––––––––––– Delivery Quarter=1986Q4 –––––––––––––––––––––––––––––

OBS	Date	Coupon	Maturity	Number Delivered	Factor
15	861231	13.125	940515	1600	1.2775
16	861231	12.625	940815	1498	1.2571
17	861231	11.750	931115	828	1.1924
18	861231	8.875	960215	9	1.0554

Total Deliveries, Average Conversion Factor = 3935   1.2513

DISCOUNT CORPORATION OF NEW YORK FUTURES
History of CBOT Note Deliveries, June 1982 To June 1988

──────────────── Delivery Quarter=1986Q3 ────────────────

OBS	Date	Coupon	Maturity	Number Delivered	Factor
19	860930	12.625	940815	4902	1.2630
20	860930	13.125	940515	2442	1.2849
21	860930	11.750	931115	1740	1.1981
22	860930	11.250	950515	140	1.1977
23	860930	11.250	950215	10	1.1933

Total Deliveries, Average Conversion Factor = 9234   1.2555

──────────────── Delivery Quarter=1986Q2 ────────────────

OBS	Date	Coupon	Maturity	Number Delivered	Factor
24	860630	11.750	931115	865	1.2030
25	860630	11.625	941115	694	1.2156
26	860630	12.625	940815	479	1.2695
27	860630	11.250	950515	326	1.2015
28	860630	11.250	950215	80	1.1977
29	860630	13.125	940515	46	1.2915
30	860630	9.500	951115	2	1.0965

Total Deliveries, Average Conversion Factor = 2492   1.2205

──────────────── Delivery Quarter=1986Q1 ────────────────

OBS	Date	Coupon	Maturity	Number Delivered	Factor
31	860331	13.125	940515	3555	1.2986
32	860331	10.500	950815	2297	1.1610
33	860331	11.250	950515	1577	1.2057
34	860331	12.625	940815	1213	1.2751
35	860331	11.625	941115	791	1.2205
36	860331	9.500	951115	761	1.0985
37	860331	11.750	931115	543	1.2085
38	860331	9.750	921015	4	1.0874
39	860324	11.250	950515	25	1.2057

Total Deliveries, Average Conversion Factor = 10766   1.2283

──────────────── Delivery Quarter=1985Q4 ────────────────

OBS	Date	Coupon	Maturity	Number Delivered	Factor
40	851231	10.50	950815	5123	1.1642
41	851231	11.25	950515	702	1.2093
42	851231	9.50	951115	21	1.1000
43	851202	10.50	950815	1	1.1642

Total Deliveries, Average Conversion Factor = 5847   1.1694

──────────────── Delivery Quarter=1985Q3 ────────────────

OBS	Date	Coupon	Maturity	Number Delivered	Factor
44	850930	11.25	950515	2981	1.2134
45	850930	10.50	950815	784	1.1668
46	850927	11.25	950515	60	1.2134

Total Deliveries, Average Conversion Factor = 3825   1.2038

──────────────── Delivery Quarter=1985Q2 ────────────────

OBS	Date	Coupon	Maturity	Number Delivered	Factor
47	850628	11.250	950515	4308	1.2169
48	850628	11.250	950215	3161	1.2134
49	850628	12.625	940815	231	1.2927
50	850627	11.250	950515	10	1.2169
51	850618	11.250	950515	447	1.2169
52	850618	11.250	950215	389	1.2134

Total Deliveries, Average Conversion Factor = 8546   1.2175

DISCOUNT CORPORATION OF NEW YORK FUTURES
History of CBOT Note Deliveries, June 1982 To June 1988   3

------------------------------ Delivery Quarter=1985Q1 ------------------------------

OBS	Date	Coupon	Maturity	Number Delivered	Factor
53	850329	11.25	950215	4166	1.2169
54	850328	11.25	950215	100	1.2169
55	850327	11.25	950215	1364	1.2169
Total Deliveries, Average Conversion Factor =				5630	1.2169

------------------------------ Delivery Quarter=1984Q4 ------------------------------

OBS	Date	Coupon	Maturity	Number Delivered	Factor
56	841231	11.625	941115	5830	1.2419

------------------------------ Delivery Quarter=1984Q3 ------------------------------

OBS	Date	Coupon	Maturity	Number Delivered	Factor
57	840928	12.625	940815	3454	1.3087
58	840927	12.625	940815	6	1.3087
59	840926	12.625	940815	1259	1.3087
Total Deliveries, Average Conversion Factor =				4719	1.3087

------------------------------ Delivery Quarter=1984Q2 ------------------------------

OBS	Date	Coupon	Maturity	Number Delivered	Factor
60	840629	13.125	940515	1256	1.3421
61	840629	11.750	931115	475	1.2416
62	840621	13.125	940515	10	1.3421
Total Deliveries, Average Conversion Factor =				1741	1.3147

------------------------------ Delivery Quarter=1984Q1 ------------------------------

OBS	Date	Coupon	Maturity	Number Delivered	Factor
63	840330	11.75	931115	3515	1.2463
64	840329	11.75	931115	10	1.2463
Total Deliveries, Average Conversion Factor =				3525	1.2463

------------------------------ Delivery Quarter=1983Q4 ------------------------------

OBS	Date	Coupon	Maturity	Number Delivered	Factor
65	831230	11.75	931115	1465	1.2503

------------------------------ Delivery Quarter=1983Q3 ------------------------------

OBS	Date	Coupon	Maturity	Number Delivered	Factor
66	830930	11.875	930815	3781	1.2586
67	830926	11.625	930815	80	1.2419
68	830921	11.625	930815	100	1.2419
69	830920	11.625	930815	349	1.2419
Total Deliveries, Average Conversion Factor =				4310	1.2566

------------------------------ Delivery Quarter=1983Q2 ------------------------------

OBS	Date	Coupon	Maturity	Number Delivered	Factor
70	830630	10.125	930515	1446	1.1417
71	830630	10.875	930215	140	1.1888
72	830629	10.125	930515	10	1.1417
73	830623	10.125	930515	13	1.1417
Total Deliveries, Average Conversion Factor =				1609	1.1458

DISCOUNT CORPORATION OF NEW YORK FUTURES
History of CBOT Note Deliveries, June 1982 To June 1988

──────────────────────────── Delivery Quarter=1983Q1 ────────────────────────────

OBS	Date	Coupon	Maturity	Number Delivered	Factor
74	830331	13.75	920515	1384	1.3640
75	830323	13.75	920515	32	1.3640
76	830322	13.75	920515	150	1.3640

Total Deliveries, Average Conversion Factor = 1566   1.3640

──────────────────────────── Delivery Quarter=1982Q4 ────────────────────────────

OBS	Date	Coupon	Maturity	Number Delivered	Factor
77	821230	13.75	920515	1124	1.3705
78	821228	13.75	920515	104	1.3705
79	821227	13.75	920515	11	1.3705
80	821220	13.75	920515	12	1.3705

Total Deliveries, Average Conversion Factor = 1251   1.3705

──────────────────────────── Delivery Quarter=1982Q3 ────────────────────────────

OBS	Date	Coupon	Maturity	Number Delivered	Factor
81	820930	13.750	920515	847	1.3776
82	820930	14.625	920215	120	1.4269
83	820924	13.750	920515	3	1.3776
84	820922	13.750	920515	93	1.3776

Total Deliveries, Average Conversion Factor = 1063   1.3832

──────────────────────────── Delivery Quarter=1982Q2 ────────────────────────────

OBS	Date	Coupon	Maturity	Number Delivered	Factor
85	820630	13.75	920515	1683	1.3839
86	820629	13.75	920515	60	1.3839
87	820628	13.75	920515	250	1.3839
88	820625	13.75	920515	500	1.3839
89	820621	13.75	920515	149	1.3839
90	820618	13.75	920515	906	1.3839
91	820615	13.75	920515	2469	1.3839

Total Deliveries, Average Conversion Factor = 6017   1.3839

Index